Bye Mam, I Love You

Bye Mam, I Love You

A daughter's last words. A mother's search for justice. The
shocking true story of the murder of Rebecca Aylward.

SONIA OATLEY

With Lynne Barrett-Lee

JOHN BLAKE

Published by John Blake Publishing Ltd,
3 Bramber Court, 2 Bramber Road,
London W14 9PB, England

www.johnblakepublishing.co.uk

www.facebook.com/johnblakebooks
twitter.com/jblakebooks

This edition published in 2014

ISBN: 978 1 78219 987 8

British Library Cataloguing-in-Publication Data:

A catalogue record for this book is available from the British Library.

Design by www.envydesign.co.uk

Printed and bound in Great Britain by CPI Group (UK) Ltd

3 5 7 9 10 8 6 4

© Text copyright Sonia Oatley and Lynne Barrett-Lee 2014

The right of Sonia Oatley and Lynne Barrett-Lee to be identified as the
authors of this work has been asserted by them in accordance with the Copyright,
Designs and Patents Act 1988.

Papers used by John Blake Publishing are natural, recyclable products made
from wood grown in sustainable forests. The manufacturing processes conform to the
environmental regulations of the country of origin.

Every attempt has been made to contact the relevant copyright-holders, but some were
unobtainable. We would be grateful if the appropriate people could contact us.

This Book is Dedicated to the Memory of my Beautiful Daughter
Rebecca Sarah Oatley

*To tell her story and share the many happy years we had
together as a family, and how every precious moment we had
together is etched in my heart and soul for eternity.*

*Our Beautiful Angel Rebecca,
We love and miss you so much and think of you
every minute of every day
We know you are always with us,
You will always be in our hearts forever
You are our light in the darkest of days
We love you more than words can say.
You will always be forever young and beautiful;
We miss you beautiful Angel x
Until we meet again x
Love you so much from Mam, Jess & Jack xxx
Let it Never be Forgot*

ACKNOWLEDGEMENTS

Rebecca – for giving me the strength to complete it; I have felt you with me every step of the way, willing me to get up in the mornings and stay strong and fight on as I know you would have done.

Jessica and Jack, my children – for understanding the need for me to write this book and giving me a hug when I needed it most xx.

Linda, my big sister – for your endless support from the moment we knew our lives would change forever.

Robert and Roger – my big brothers who looked after us all, Mam and Dad would be so proud of you.

My Lorraines – who were and still are always there for me.

Linda and Marcus Roberts – your support, especially through the trial, meant so much to us, and Marcus, who Becca always talked fondly about, she would have been so proud of you for being so brave.

Kayleigh, Nia Bethan and Lauren (Becca's friends) – who she loved dearly and I know will always look after you x.

Lynne Barrett-Lee, my wordsmith – for her feedback and enthusiastic support, and who always offered great advice! A professional author throughout with all the sadness and difficulties we had to endure, who helped me write this book and provided the perfect blend of knowledge and skills that went into authoring this book. I thank you for devoting your time and effort towards it.

Andrew Lownie, my agent – for all his hard work in the publishing of this book.

John Blake Publishing – for having faith in me and helping me tell Rebecca's story.

My editor, Chris Mitchell – words cannot express my gratitude for his professional advice and assistance in polishing this manuscript. And thanks also to the illustrator and book designers.

Christopher Heath – for restoring my faith and giving me words of validation from my Angel Rebecca.

St Mary's and St Patrick's RC School – the primary school that Rebecca, Jessica and Jack attended. All the staff who supported us in so many ways through the worst time of our lives.

John Doherty and Charmaine Kinson, our Family Liaison Officers – for their professionalism throughout, their understanding of our emotions and supporting us every step of the way.

Gareth Watts, the funeral directors – for their kindness and the delicate way they handled the funeral arrangements.

To everyone who supported us throughout – your cards,

ACKNOWLEDGEMENTS

letters and kind words and for encouraging me to write this book I thank each and every one of you.

To all my new friends (way too many to mention but you know who you are) who sadly have lost loved ones in similarly tragic circumstances to us, living the same nightmare, the endless sleepless nights, the tears that never stop falling, the piece of your heart that will always be missing.

Without you all and your encouragement to keep going and telling me to stay strong for Becca this book would not have been possible.

Thank you.

CONTENTS

PART ONE

CHAPTER ONE

BACK TOGETHER

There is an instinct, I think, that exists in every mother. A sixth sense that tells you something bad has happened to your child, no matter how much people try to reassure you otherwise.

It was 7.30pm on Saturday, 23 October 2010 and my brother Roger's phone battery had just died. I had been using it to call the police, trying to report my eldest daughter Becca missing and, frustratingly, had been cut off mid-sentence. I had no other phone I could use to call back either. We'd only moved into our new house in Maesteg, Bridgend, nine days previously and the landline wasn't being connected till Monday. The only other phone I had was Becca's iPhone and that had no credit, which was why she'd taken my BlackBerry out with her instead – I didn't want her going out with no way of getting in touch and my BlackBerry was on contract. It was a bit of a thing with me and always had been. From a very young age I'd instilled a set of instructions in the children – had them memorise both our home number and their Auntie Linda's number, and made sure they knew how to make a reverse-charge call.

Nevertheless, Becca hadn't been in contact for six hours now, which was completely unlike her. She was a good girl. Reliable. She always answered my calls. The fact that this time she hadn't done so meant that something must have happened to the phone, or to her.

'Oh, God,' I said, staring at the screen. 'I don't believe it! We need to go to Linda's house and call them back from there,' I told my brother as I grabbed my coat and bag. 'The sooner we do that, the sooner they can go out and start looking for her, can't they? This is just so not like her.'

My other daughter, Jess, was out looking for Becca, and Jack, my youngest, kept asking, 'Where is she, Mam?'

'Maybe she's at Josh's gran's house. Remember, there's no signal there,' I reminded them. But though this was true, I had still felt sick with anxiety. The only reason I knew there wasn't a signal was precisely because Becca was so responsible; back when she was dating Josh before, she'd taken the trouble to call and tell me, so I wouldn't worry if she went out of range. So if she'd been going there, she would have texted or called to tell me again because she wouldn't have wanted me worrying. That was how she was.

My brother held the door open and we trooped out of the house into the bitter night. 'She should keep in touch,' he was saying. 'Putting you through all this... When she does get finally get home, you should ground her for a month.'

As if... I remember thinking that, even then. When she came home I wouldn't shout at her – I'd hug her. Hug her tight. I was so anxious right now that I knew I'd find it hard to ever let her out of my sight again. My brother didn't know her like I did. How could he? He wasn't her mam. This was my Becca and that simply wasn't the kind of girl she was.

I kept trying to reassure Jack all the way to my sister's. She'd come home, I kept telling him. She'd be home before he knew it. But you know sometimes, don't you? When things are not right, you just know it. Yet you dare not admit it – not to anyone, yourself included. Because if you do then your worst fears might come true.

The scent of pink-rose bubble bath had lingered in the hallway all day that Saturday, from when I'd run Becca a bath at 6.30 that morning. She'd been up so early and, having heard her, I decided I'd get up too, so I could make sure the heating was on and run her a bath. She hadn't been able to sleep a wink, she'd told me as she joined me in the bathroom – she'd been much too excited about the coming day. 'Oh, Mam,' I remember her saying with a giggle as she eyed the water. 'That won't even cover my knees!'

She'd turned the taps on then and filled the bath right up to the top. I hadn't minded – it was a big day for her, after all. The Josh she'd gone to meet that day was Joshua Davies, an ex-boyfriend of hers from several months back. He'd been in touch again recently and she was hoping they might get back together. She'd been heartbroken when he'd ended the relationship back in January, so I hoped so too. Like any mother, I had the usual reservations about it, though. Josh had always seemed a nice boy – we'd known him since they both started in high school – but I still worried that he might break her heart again.

Jack, on the other hand, was almost as excited about seeing Josh as Becca was. He always looked forward to Josh coming up because they would spend time playing games or going to the park. I felt differently, however, as any mother would. Yes, I'd be civil but I still remembered how much he'd hurt her when he broke up with her; he'd have to do some work to regain my trust.

'Mam, you will be nice to him if he comes up on the weekend, won't you?' Becca had asked me earlier in the week. And I'd answered truthfully, reminding her about the nasty MSN messages he'd sent her after he'd finished with her. Yes, I would be civil but I wasn't going to make it that easy for him. I wanted him to know he was still on probation.

I knew my sister Linda felt the same. Fourteen years older than me, Linda was the eldest of my siblings – I also had two older brothers, Robert and Roger. Since Mam had died in 1994 – only three years after our father passed away – she'd been like a second mother to us too. She was the lynchpin of the family, not only looking after my eldest brother Robert, who'd been unwell for several years, but also a wonderful support when I split up with my ex-husband.

Linda and I were as close as any sisters could be. And with no children of her own – she'd been married to her job as a senior midwife – she was really like a grandmother to my three children. She idolised them and always had; she'd been a big part their childhood. And it was going fast. Jessica, my second daughter, was 13 now and we could both hardly believe Jack was 9. Needless to say, all three of them adored Linda too and we'd spend many hours together, having fun.

Linda liked to spoil them rotten as well. Only the day before, she'd taken Becca shopping in Cardiff for new clothes for her 'date' and, as I didn't drive myself, had agreed she'd play chauffeur today as well – as Josh apparently 'didn't do buses' – telling Becca to call her as soon as she was ready and that she'd come over and collect her, giving me time to continue with the unpacking from our move. She'd then go shopping with Jess till Becca and Josh were ready and bring them back, so Josh could sleep over at ours.

But as the morning wore on, I began fretting. Yes, the plans had been made but there was silence from Josh. Becca had been trying to get hold of him all morning because she'd not heard a word from him, either by phone or text. They'd arranged everything during the week but why the sudden silence? Was he messing her about all over again?

It seemed so but I tried to reassure Becca.

'You know what boys are like,' I told her. 'He's probably still in bed.' Josh would often stay in bed till 1pm, I remembered. And then, as if on cue, he *did* text her, and she was happy again and immediately phoned Linda to come and pick her up. Becca was still anxious that one of her siblings come with her, however; she'd even suggested to Jack that they take one of Josh's younger brothers, Jake, to the park so that they could all play on the swings. Jake and our Jack were around the same age and, though they didn't know each other that well – they attended different primary schools – Jake had been over to our house a few times and Jack to his. Before Becca and Josh's break-up, I would treat both boys as if they were almost part of the family; they were so close that I would even make the effort to get their favourite treats in if I knew they were

7

coming round – we were that sort of family. I'd think nothing of pulling out the barbecue and doing an impromptu party for all the kids' friends.

'Come with me, Jack?' Becca had been asking him that morning. '*Please?*' He had finally agreed, the night before, that he *would* go with her and Linda. But this morning he'd changed his mind again and decided to do something else. At the time I wasn't really sure why she was so bothered about him going anyway but she clearly was. She'd even tried to get Jessica to go with her too, which had struck me as odd. I thought she'd want to be alone with Josh, and so I said so.

'I'm just a bit nervous,' she explained. 'It's been such a long time since I've seen him alone – there's always been one of the girls with me. Make one of them come with me, Mam, *please!*'

I'd told her it wasn't fair to make them go if they didn't want to, although I did ask them again for her. But again they said no: they had their own plans. But Becca seemed OK with it in the end, especially once she'd finally heard from Josh; by now she was more excited than nervous. So while we waited for Linda, they switched the TV to one of the music channels and, as I carried on unpacking boxes, I could hear them all singing – and no doubt dancing as well – in the other room.

'Mam, red or green?' Becca asked me once we knew Linda was on her way. She was holding up two Superdry lumber jackets. 'Which one looks best, do you think?' she asked, laughing, as she tried them both on.

They were new. Linda had treated the girls the day before when they went to Cardiff shopping and, as they often shared clothes, Jessica said she didn't mind which one Becca took. After much debate, I decided upon the red one. 'Because you have the royal-blue Hollister T-shirt on,' I told her, 'and it goes better with the red Superdry.' Though, in truth, Becca was so petite and had such a lovely figure that she looked good in anything she wore.

As Linda pulled up outside, Jessica agreed with me, and so Becca donned it happily, along with her new brown ankle boots. She'd bought them the previous day, especially for the occasion, together with a little matching new brown shoulder bag. 'And here's some money,' I told her. 'To get some pizzas or whatever you and Josh want for tonight.'

She picked up her handbag and slipped my BlackBerry and the cash into it. 'See you in a bit,' she said, giving me a kiss and hug. 'Bye Mam, I love you!'

'Love you too, babes,' I told her as I kissed and hugged her back. 'See you in a bit.'

I watched them go, my two daughters, laughing and chatting as they walked down to Linda's waiting car. Then, just before they climbed in, they both turned to wave. Becca looked so happy, I remember thinking. Then she was gone.

I used the next hour or so productively. With us having moved into the house so recently, there was still a lot of unpacking to be done and, with Josh coming over for a sleepover, I particularly wanted the place to be straight. I'd sort some bedding out, I remember thinking, so he could sleep on the sofa; they'd probably sit up late watching films and playing games on the Xbox with Jess and Jack while I cooked them all their favourite food.

It was strange to think of him being back in our lives again and when Becca had asked me if he could come for a sleepover, I'd refused at first. But she really wanted him to come and was at pains to convince me. 'He's OK now,' she told me. 'He's back to the old Josh again.' And she was so happy that in the end I caved in. Once I'd done so, I tried to think like Becca – she saw the good in absolutely everyone. And if she wanted to give him a second chance, I thought, so should I, even though I knew he'd eat me out of house and home.

Josh had a huge appetite and whenever he'd come round previously – often turning up straight after school, having come on the school bus with the others – he'd make a beeline for the kitchen to see what I was cooking. His favourite was chips, two eggs, four sausages and a full packet of bacon, with beans on the side and sometimes bread and butter too. 'That smells nice, Son,' he'd say to me, poking his nose in while I was cooking and telling me how I cooked the bacon exactly the way he liked it – burned almost to a cinder. Something he apparently never got at home. Josh didn't so much eat as demolish a plate of food – he ate more like an animal than any boy I'd ever known.

I was miles away when Becca's iPhone rang – I had it on me, so it startled me. Then I remembered that, with no credit on it, I couldn't make a call myself but I could still receive one. Of course, I thought, seeing it was just after 1pm, it would be Becca herself, to tell me they were all on their way back with Josh.

But that wasn't the case. 'I'm in Pandy Park,' she told me. 'I'm still waiting for him.'

'Pandy Park?' I said, confused. Why on earth would she be there? 'That wasn't where you were supposed to meet him. What are you doing there?' I asked her.

She explained that there had been a change of plan; that his parents, Hayley and Steve, wanted to see her apparently and that they'd now be going there for a while. She didn't seem to know why they were so anxious to meet her and it seemed a little odd to me too. And it certainly didn't explain why she was made to meet him in Pandy Park.

'Why there?' I asked again.

'He wouldn't say,' Becca answered. 'He just told me not to let anyone see me.'

'Why ever not?' I asked, irritated at this silly teenage obsession with secrecy. I'd always liked Josh – he'd always been such a nice, polite boy – but he'd been just like this when they'd been together before, saying things like 'you never saw me' as if he was part of some great MI5 spy ring or something. It was as if she was some sort of guilty secret – either that or he felt embarrassed to be going out with her. It made no sense to me: 'Why does he want you to hide all the time, Bec?'

I heard her sigh. 'I don't know, Mam, but I'm *really* fed up now! I've been waiting here for *ages*! I just saw Santa [Santa was the nickname for Josh's other young brother, Jordan] but I couldn't let him see me.'

This *really* annoyed me. *For goodness sake*, I thought. *He'd already told her his mum and dad had wanted to see her, so why was she supposed to pretend she wasn't there?* 'Why ever not?' I said again.

'Because Josh said he mustn't. Oh, and I also saw Josh Humphreys,' she added. 'He was out walking his dog.'

Josh Humphreys was a nice boy and a good friend of Becca's. She'd seen a lot of him over the summer when they dated for a while and they still got on well but with Josh Davies hinting they might get back together, she'd finished seeing Josh Humphreys – as a boyfriend, at least – a little while back.

'So did you speak to *him*?' I asked her.

'No, but I think I might go and see him. I did phone Lauren to see if I could go to her house but there's no answer.' She sighed again. 'I really am fed up now, Mam. Where *is* he?' *And why is he doing this?*

Like any mother would, I felt really anxious now. And I was so cross with Josh – why did he need her to meet him in the park, anyway? It was such an out-of-the-way place, and I didn't like Becca being there alone. And why was he so late coming to meet her? What was he playing at?

'I don't want you hanging around in the park on your own, love,' I told Becca. 'Phone him now and tell him you're going to walk back to the village. I'd feel happier if you were there – there'll be plenty of people around. Or why don't you just walk to Josh's house anyway? If his parents said they wanted to see you, they'll probably be there, won't they? And so might Josh be. And he might be trying to call you anyway. Why don't you call him again? And then ring me straight back, OK?'

It was only a matter of half a minute before Becca phoned again. 'It's OK,' she said and I could hear that she was walking quickly now. 'I spoke to him and I'm on my way to meet him over in Church Street. I'm walking over the bridge now, heading into the tunnel, but there are some boys in a car near the park that I don't like the look of...'

'Go on then, quickly,' I urged her, feeling even more anxious with all this talk of tunnels and suspicious-looking boys. 'I'll stay on the phone till you meet up with Josh.'

Which was what I did; I kept talking to her, asking who was

about. I didn't like my children to be out on their own, any of them, and I hated knowing she was alone in the park, even though it was a bright Saturday afternoon, particularly if she was walking through a tunnel. It was a kind of underpass, she explained to me as she walked, very cold and very dark. 'Mam,' she said breathlessly. She was clearly hurrying, as I'd told her. 'Can you hear me echoing?'

'Hurry,' I told her. 'I don't like you being in there.'

'It's OK,' she said. 'Don't worry, Mam. There's a policewoman walking behind me.'

'Really?' I felt sure she was just saying this to reassure me – it would be so like her. She knew how I fretted.

'Yes,' she said firmly. 'Honestly, there is.'

'Put her on then,' I said.

'Oh, Mam, *really?*' she teased me.

'Yes,' I said. 'Really.'

'OK,' she began. 'If you really, really want me to...'

'No, you're all right,' I said, feeling a bit silly. It was the middle of the day, after all – I mustn't let my imagination run away with me.

'I'm out of the park now, in any case,' she told me. 'Just going past Josh's street now.'

These plans seemed so ridiculous. Why couldn't she just meet him on his own road? So I said so. 'Why up on Church Street?' I asked her. 'Isn't he at his house? What's he playing at?'

I heard Becca sigh. 'I don't *know* but I'm pretty fed up now.'

This was getting ridiculous. 'Look,' I said, 'phone Linda. Go and meet her and Jessica. Why on earth is he making you run around all over Aberkenfig and making you hide from all his family and friends?'

'It's OK, Mam. I'm going up Church Street—'

'Well, I hope he hurries up and meets you. We've got hail here and it's heading your way – you'll get soaked.'

'There are hailstones here too,' she said. 'But it's OK, I've got my hood up. I'm under a tree now, anyway.'

'Under a *tree*? Where exactly?'

'Up by Church Street, by a cemetery – it's not very nice. It's scary being in a cemetery all on my own.'

'It's fine,' I reassured her. 'It's living people you need to be scared of. Not dead people, silly. Dead people can't harm you.'

She agreed I was right but I was becoming increasingly anxious myself. What *was* he playing at? I was beginning to get really angry with him now, sick of him messing my daughter around like this. 'Don't worry,' I reassured her. 'You're not on your own – I'll stay on the phone till Josh arrives. Any sign of him yet?'

'No, not yet...' She seemed to stop and think then. 'He'd better not be bringing Ninnis!'

Daniel Ninnis was Josh's best friend – had been since nursery school. And since Becca had turned him down when he'd asked to go out with her himself, he hadn't liked her and was invariably unpleasant whenever they met. He also, I knew, had said some horrible things about her. No wonder Becca wasn't keen on seeing him; she didn't like him at all.

'Well, if he does,' I said, 'just phone Linda and come home again, OK?'

'It's OK, Mam. I'll be... Oh, it's OK... There's Josh! He's walking down the hill now.'

Finally, I thought, wanting to give him a piece of my mind. Despite his silly nonsense, I'd always warmed to Josh because he'd always seemed such a nice boy, really. But I wasn't happy at all that he'd kept Becca waiting in the middle of nowhere for so long – particularly seeing as the one thing he always used to say when they'd gone out together previously was, 'She's safe with me – don't worry. I'll always protect her!'

'Josh Davies?' I asked, suddenly realising Becca might have meant Josh Humphreys. 'I don't want to ring off unless I'm a hundred per cent sure it's Josh Davies. You're with him now? Definitely?'

She laughed. 'Of course I'm sure, Mam! He's standing right here in front of me, right now.'

But I couldn't hear him, which was weird because normally I'd expect to. He was a confident boy, a noisy boy, always the centre of attention, always joking around. Whenever I spoke to Becca in school – if she called me during break, say – his would always be one of the voices I could hear in the background; laughing, joining in like teenagers do, saying, 'Hiya, Son!' Or even taking the phone out of her hand so he could have a chat with me as well.

But today he said nothing. I listened hard but it was as if he wasn't even there. I remember noticing he didn't make a sound. Why ever not?

'OK,' I said, having no choice but to believe my daughter. 'I'll see you later then. But how are you going to get home now? What about Linda?'

'Don't worry,' Becca said. 'Hayley [Josh's mother] will bring us back up later.' And if they were going there, it did make sense – more sense than Linda and Jessica hanging around for them. 'Bye Mam,' Becca finished then, 'I love you.'

'See you later,' I replied. And, as always, I said, 'I love you too.'

It was the last time I ever spoke to my baby.

CHAPTER TWO

WHERE'S BECCA?

My sister Linda lived in Llangynwyd, a distance of about four miles from where we had just moved to, and as we rushed to her house to finish making the phone call that evening, the events of the afternoon kept replaying in my mind.

It was Linda who'd first been concerned for Becca's safety. She'd called me mid-afternoon, having returned home with Jessica, to alert me to the fact that Becca hadn't rung her to arrange picking up her and Josh. She also told me that, although Becca had spoken to Jessica briefly (and had said that she was with Josh at his house at the time), she was no longer answering her phone.

'She isn't coming home tonight. I just know it,' she told me.

'Of course she is,' I reassured her, not understanding what she meant. I then told her about what Becca had said about Josh's mum perhaps bringing them home. 'Besides,' I added, 'If she'd thought there was a chance she might sleep over, she'd have taken her make-up and spare clothes, wouldn't she?'

But hearing about Hayley didn't seem to calm Linda. And I was shocked by how agitated she still seemed. 'I just have a bad feeling about all this, Sonia,' she told me.

'Stop worrying,' I said. 'She was with Josh when I spoke to her. She'll be fine with him – he always looks after her.'

'That may be so,' she answered, 'but Sonia, we can't just do nothing. It's four o'clock now, for goodness sake! Why isn't she answering? She *always* answers her phone and it's been *ages* since we heard from her. And they were supposed to be coming back with us, so why didn't Becca call me and tell me that? Don't you find that odd? I just think we should call around so we know where she is. Tell you what – you have her phone there, so why don't you give me the numbers of all her friends, then I can start trying to track her down from here.'

I felt flustered now, made more anxious by my sister's agitated tone. 'You'll have to ring me back in a few minutes then,' I told her, cursing that I had no landline to use when I needed it – cursing that I was on the phone Becca might be trying to contact me on right that very minute. 'I'll get some paper – give me a chance to get them off the phone and write them down for you.'

I used Becca's pen to do it, one of those multi-coloured ballpoints. I used the pink ink – Becca's favourite – and duly made the list. And as I was doing so, I underlined both Davies's and Ninnis's names and numbers, though in the end, when I called Linda back, I didn't bother giving her Ninnis's. What would be the point? Becca didn't like him – was scared of him even – so he'd be the last person she'd be with, wouldn't he?

I left Linda to make the calls then and tried to get on with unpacking the rest of the boxes that still littered the living room. Stupid, perhaps, but I wanted the place to look nice before Josh arrived; it would be the first time he'd visited our new home and I knew Becca would be keen to make a good impression. Jack was upstairs playing and I wondered about calling him down to help me but, having decided he had enough things to sort out in his own room, I rolled up my sleeves, determined to press on with it. However, although I still thought that Linda was probably worrying unnecessarily (after all, Becca had always got on with Josh's parents, so could be there for ages), I could no longer concentrate; not now that seed of anxiety had been sown. It *was* odd that Becca hadn't at least called Linda to fill her in. And it was 5pm now, almost dark.

Linda called again, as promised, at around 6pm. And as soon as I heard her voice, I felt a jolt of fresh anxiety. Now she sounded even more worried than before.

'I've spoken to Josh's father,' she told me. 'And he says he hasn't seen either of them.'

'What? Are you *sure?*' I asked, shocked. I didn't understand – how could that be? 'Was he actually *at* home, though?' I asked. 'Might he have missed them earlier on?'

'No,' Linda said. 'He told me he'd been in all afternoon so they obviously didn't go there. So where *did* they go?'

All these changes of plan, I thought. *Why?* And why hadn't Becca called to let me know? It was so unlike her. But still I rationalised that there would be a reason for all the mystery and it was at this point that I remembered Josh's grandmother. 'Perhaps they went to Josh's gran's house instead,' I suggested to Linda. 'That might be the reason her phone's not answering.'

As Becca had said before, there was barely any phone signal in Shwt, where his gran lived. *Yes, that must be it*, I thought, feeling a little calmer. That would explain it, that would be why she couldn't call.

I said so, but Linda didn't agree. She was worried, she said, because everything just felt wrong about it. And she was also anxious that we take action now. 'You need to call the police,' she said, which frightened me. The *police*? Why the police? What was she so anxious about? It all seemed so drastic.

'Because no one's seen or heard *anything*,' she said grimly. 'It's like she's just vanished.'

I felt the fear start creeping through me then – a sense of cold dread that I'd so far been trying to think myself out of, but which now coiled inside me like liquid ice. How could *no one* have a clue where she was, no one at all? Surely she would have texted *someone*, at some point?

'We're going to go out and look for her,' Linda told me finally. 'I'm going to take Jess and Shannon [Shannon was a good friend of both the girls] and we're going to drive to a few of her friends' houses – see if anyone else has heard from her. See if she's texted or called in on anyone at any point. And if not, we'll head up to MacArthur Glen and see if she's there. I'll ring you as soon as we have any news.'

'But I want to come with you,' I protested. 'I can't just wait here and do nothing!'

'You have to,' Linda said, 'for the meanwhile, at least. You need to stay there in case she calls or the police turn up, needing information. We'll look everywhere, I promise. And I'll call you the minute I have news.'

But there hadn't been any news. Everywhere they went, they drew a blank: they'd called at numerous friends' houses and had gone to MacArthur Glen, just as Linda had said. They'd gone to all the shops Becca liked going in and trailed around the food court. They'd even gone to the security office and had asked the security guard to put a call out for Becca on the tannoy. They waited 10 minutes after that, just as the lady had suggested, and when Becca didn't show, they then drove all around Aberkenfig, checking all the places they knew Becca and Josh might go. Finally, they went to Sarn, where Josh Humphreys lived and where Josh Davies had apparently told Becca to meet him. Meanwhile, Jack and I, without a working phone to use, could do nothing but wait till they returned with news and just sit by Becca's iPhone, willing it to ring.

I called the police at 7.15pm to report Becca missing.

Linda and the girls, meanwhile, had also been to Josh Humphreys' house and, finding no one at home and the house in complete darkness, Jess and Shannon had even found a way into their back garden just in case Becca was there. But she hadn't been and, as my brother and Jack and I drove to Linda's to finish the aborted phone conversation, Linda and the girls made another circuit of all the places they'd previously been to, just in case they had missed seeing her the first time.

I finished giving the police the details and was told I would have to wait for a return phone call, at which point they'd arrange to send somebody round. Another wait. Another frustration too – how long would they be? It was getting so late now! But at least I now had a working phone, so I used it. I tried Becca constantly and, in between, tried Josh Davies –

neither of which number connected. I also tried Josh Humphreys, but every time I called him, he would answer and say hello, then once I told him who I was, straight away he'd hang up again. Why would he do that?

I called Steve again too, Josh Davies's father, and he told me the same as he'd told Linda earlier on – that, no, he hadn't seen Becca at any point in the afternoon and that he hadn't seen Josh either. He was adamant that Josh had been at his gran's house and, as far as he knew, he was still up there with his mates.

'Can I have her number then?' I asked him, as he didn't offer it. He duly gave it to me and I called Josh's gran as soon as I put down the phone. It was now approaching 9pm – eight whole hours since we'd last seen or heard from my daughter. But she would surely, *surely*, be able to tell us something.

'Is Josh there?' I asked, after I explained who I was. My heart was thumping and I tried to keep my voice level.

'He's upstairs with his friends,' she confirmed. *Finally.* Now I might at last get some answers. 'Can you call him then, please?' I asked. 'I need to speak to him as a matter of urgency.'

I heard her call up to him then; heard her say, 'Becca's mother is on the phone,' followed by the sound of him mumbling some response I couldn't hear, then him telling her, 'I'll take it up here.'

The phone clicked and at last I was speaking to him. I took a deep breath, trying to keep myself calm. 'Hiya, Josh,' I said. 'Have you seen Becca at all today? Only we can't get in touch with her.' There was a pause.

'No, Son,' he said at length. 'I haven't seen her.'

'OK,' I said, trying to quell my alarm on hearing this. 'But didn't you and Becca plan to come to our house today?'

'Erm, yeah,' he said after another pause, 'but I got stuck at my gran's house and couldn't get to Aberkenfig for another two hours, so she told me she'd go and kill the time with Josh Humphreys. That's where she is, with that Josh Humphreys kid.'

That did make some sense, I thought, remembering what Becca had said about her seeing Josh Humphreys. But what about Josh Davies – the boy who was on the phone to me *now*? The boy who Becca had said had actually been walking towards her, the last time we'd spoken on the phone? *That* made no sense to me at all.

'Listen, Josh,' I said, 'when I spoke to Becca on the phone earlier, she was waiting for you in Church Street. She even said to me, "Oh, here he is now, coming down the hill towards me." Are you telling me you weren't standing in front of her while she was on the phone to me?'

Another pause. Then he said, 'No.'

'But Josh,' I persisted, 'I asked her three times if it was you and she was a hundred per cent sure it was. Are you saying it wasn't? Are you *really* saying she's with Josh Humphreys?'

'She must be,' he said again – very clearly and very slowly. He didn't sound at all like I remembered him, I realised. He was a boy who talked a lot and talked quickly, rushing to get the words out, but not today. Today, the spaces between his words gaped.

'OK,' I said. 'Thanks. Josh, can you do me a favour? Can you ask around your friends for me? Ask if any of them have seen her and let me know? The police are involved now and want to hear from anyone who might have seen her. Can you do that?'

He told me he would.

It was only afterwards that it struck me how strange it was that he should still be at his gran's. Two hours, he'd said. He'd told Becca at lunchtime he'd be held up for two hours, that was all. And yet he was still there. He hadn't even returned to Aberkenfig and had made no mention to me at any point of having been out trying to find her. Why? Because he didn't care that she was missing, or because he knew her whereabouts only too well?

The police officers arrived at Linda's just after 9.30pm, it making more sense for them to come to her house as she had a working phone. They were full of apologies that it had taken them so long to get to us but explained that they had had a particularly busy evening, due to it being the first night of half term.

Linda showed them in and, while Robert took Jess and Jack into the kitchen, we were asked to go through all the details of the last times we'd seen and spoken to Becca.

There were two police officers – a very tall man who wrote in a notebook and a young female officer who sat on the sofa with Linda and asked questions. But I couldn't sit down myself. I was too frantic to sit still and had to pace the room as I answered, having to describe Becca's height and build and tell them what she'd been wearing, and getting agitated at what seemed to be pointless, time-wasting questions about what sort of girl she was and whether she'd 'done this sort of thing' before.

'After all, it's the first night of half term,' the male officer repeated. 'She's probably just at one of the parties that are going on.'

I knew they had to ask but it was beginning to feel as if my answers weren't being listened to: that she wouldn't be at *any* party – she'd planned a night in at home with a movie; that she didn't drink and that she always, *always* answered her phone; that even if she had decided to go to a party, she would have called me and asked permission; that she just wasn't irresponsible like that.

'What school does she go to?' the officer asked then.

'Archbishop McGrath,' I told him.

And as soon as I said this, the two police officers exchanged glances.

'We've just picked up a drunk teenage girl,' the woman explained, 'another pupil at Archbishop. So perhaps the party she was at will be as good a place to start looking as any. We'll head back down there now,' she said, getting up from the sofa. 'Have you got a recent picture of Becca we can take with us?'

I pulled out her phone and found one, which I showed the police officer, all the while thinking what a complete waste of time their going there was. There was no way she'd be there – not willingly.

By now, having seen them out, I was frantic. Yes, they were out looking for her, but in all the wrong places and there seemed little I could do but let them get on with it till they'd reached that conclusion themselves.

That they would, indeed, reach the same conclusion I was not in any doubt. Becca didn't just avoid drink because she was a responsible 15-year-old; she didn't touch it because she'd been so ill over the summer – something that, as yet, hadn't even been resolved. She'd had chronic but totally inexplicable stomach problems and dizzy spells, and more than once had completely blacked out. Back in July she'd even been hospitalised and had undergone MRI scans, blood tests and sleep-deprivation tests, none of which had brought us nearer to an explanation.

Was that it? Had she blacked out? Was she lying somewhere, unconscious? Linda and I looked at each other helplessly. Surely the police could do more? Why couldn't they get a helicopter out? That angered me greatly. They had them out all the time, didn't they, chasing kids in stolen cars? Why not for my baby, out there all alone?

I tried to calm myself, seeing the fear in both Jack and Jess's faces when they returned from the kitchen. 'It's OK,' I told them. 'The police are on to it now – they're going to go and find Becca and bring her home safe to us.'

I tried to believe it too, hard though it seemed, having seen the police officers, and hearing all their talk about parties and the sort of things they assumed *all* teenagers did.

In any case I didn't care what Becca might have done – I never had. I just wanted her home safe with me. But all I had was her phone, which remained stubbornly silent and which I kept picking up and ringing. But it was always with the same result – nothing. It would just ring and ring and ring, or, with so many other people probably ringing it, one time in ten it would go straight to voicemail – that cool recorded voice, which felt so at odds with the whirring of my brain.

The police returned to Linda's house just before midnight but despite my praying and praying she would be with them, Becca wasn't there. And their first news was equally negative: it turned out that Becca wasn't with Josh Humphreys. They'd traced him to a club in Ogmore Vale, apparently, and it seemed the reason for his manner when I'd been trying to talk to him on the phone had simply been because the music was so loud that he'd been unable to hear anything I'd been saying.

Nor had the police made any progress in finding out where Becca might be instead. 'But try not to worry,' they told me. 'There's another party we've just been told about in Ogmore Vale. We'll try there next.'

Which seemed insane. I knew Becca would never have gone to a party there, and so I said so. It was quite a rough area, in places, and it was also where a girl called Mini – Josh Davies's last girlfriend – lived. I was desperate to feel they were doing something more focused than just driving around from party to party in any case; parties where I knew they would not find my daughter.

'What about CCTV?' I suggested. 'Couldn't you check that? And what about Josh Davies and his parents? Have you been to see them?' Just before the police had arrived, Josh's father had called to see if he could help search and, as I didn't know Aberkenfig well enough to suggest where he should look, I'd asked him to ask Josh where might be a good idea to go. I told the police this and they noted it but still they didn't tell me anything further and I didn't even think to ask.

'Or how about mobile-phone signal?' I suggested instead. I was still focused on them tracking her somehow. 'Or can't you call out a heat-seeking helicopter and track her through that?'

I knew this was something that could be done but they shook their heads. 'That's not possible, I'm afraid,' the male officer told me. 'We can only call for a helicopter after twenty-four hours have passed, or if the missing person has a medical condition.'

Of course I leapt on this and immediately told them about

Becca's blackouts and hospitalisation, frightening myself anew in the process. Was that what had happened, that she had suffered another blackout? Was she lying unconscious somewhere even as we spoke?

But even though they wrote it down, still they shook their heads and I couldn't believe how calm they were, how relaxed they seemed to be. Despite everything I'd told them about the sort of girl Becca was, it was as if the only explanation they still thought worth considering was that she'd gone off to some party and failed to tell me.

'But when we finish our shifts,' they reassured me, 'we'll make the other shift aware of what's happening.'

Or not happening, I thought. *Why weren't they doing more? Didn't they care that there was a 15-year-old girl out there, perhaps alone?*

It seemed not because I didn't hear another word from either shift then and it was left to me to call for updates, which I did on an hourly basis, only to be told that there was nothing new to report. They didn't even ask for the number of the mobile so that they could try to get in touch with her themselves.

It was incredibly frustrating. My brother Roger kept telling me to leave the police to do their job but both Linda and I disagreed. They *weren't* doing their job. What exactly *had* they done? To us it felt like very little – so far, all they'd done was to go and look for her at two parties I'd already told them she wouldn't be at.

By this time, Roger and his wife Janet had taken Jess home with them, just in case Becca turned up there. Jack and I, meanwhile, stayed at Linda's with my older brother, Robert, so I could be on hand if the police needed to speak to me. Finally

I managed to get Jack off to sleep on the sofa but, as the minutes of the night inched their way inexorably round, I didn't quite know what to do with myself. My mind was racing. Why hadn't they called? Why hadn't there been any news? Were they taking *any* of this seriously? It seemed to me the only ones doing anything were Becca's friends, who had all been busy posting messages on Facebook trying to find her and texting round to see if anyone had seen or heard from her. All her friends, that was, bar Josh Davies himself, who appeared to have done nothing to help. He'd not even phoned me to see if there'd been any news about her.

Not once.

At around 2am Jack woke up and his first words to me were, 'Mam, is Becca home yet?' He'd been dreaming of her, apparently, and had thought she'd come home.

'Not yet, babes,' I told him. 'But she will be soon, don't worry.' Then I lay down beside him to try and coax him back to sleep.

And I must have fallen asleep too at some point because the next thing that happened was that I was woken with a jolt, at 3am. And I did what you do when you're woken up in such circumstances – I thought I'd dreamed it, every single bit of it. But then the room came into focus and I realised it was still happening and the panic inside me rose all over again.

Three in the morning – God, where *was* she? Unable to bear the oppressive darkness, I eased myself carefully from Jack so I wouldn't wake him, then rushed to the front door and opened it. It was so *cold*, I remember thinking. Was she out there somewhere in this temperature? I stepped outside into the frosty air, trying to quell my terror, and all I could keep thinking, as the tears streamed down my cheeks, was that it was *so* bitterly cold out there and my baby was out there somewhere. Like any mother, I needed to be feeling whatever Becca was feeling. It couldn't help find her right now but at least I could do that.

I don't think I had ever felt so alone as I did at that moment. It seemed to me the whole world was sleeping, but how could they do that when my little girl was out there somewhere? How had I let this happen? I should wake everyone, shouldn't I – everyone who loved her? We should be down there – forget letting the police do their job. We should be down in Aberkenfig with the police, helping to look for her. Where *was* everyone? Was I the only one awake and terrified for my little girl? Because I'd never been so terrified, ever.

CHAPTER THREE

A MOTHER'S
INSTINCT

For the rest of the night I didn't sleep a wink. It was such a long night, and such a dark night in so many ways, and I spent the remainder of it pacing. Still I kept trying the BlackBerry but still there was nothing – just the slight leap of faith I felt when it went straight to voicemail – was she on it? Was she trying to text me? Trying to ring me?

But each time that hope morphed into an ever-increasing panic, as terrifying images repeatedly flooded my mind. Might she be calling for me? Needing my help? Perhaps she was lying injured somewhere. Could someone have abducted her and taken her phone off her? I couldn't bear feeling so helpless but I had no idea what to do.

Get a grip, I kept telling myself. *Blank the thoughts out. Try to think straight.* But however hard I tried, back they'd come; horrible picture upon horrible picture, as all the 'what ifs' lined up to torment me.

After that last call to the police, hours ago, I'd heard nothing. All I knew – and I didn't even know that, not really – was that a new shift had started at 3am and was to continue where the last one had left off. But what *were* they doing? Anything? I had no idea. There had been no updates, no phone calls, nothing. I didn't know what they were doing right *then*, let alone what their plan of action might be.

At 7am, going mad with the waiting and hoping, I took myself off into the dining room with Linda's phone and dialled the number for Bridgend Police Station.

'I'm sorry,' the woman said. 'I haven't anything to tell you, I'm afraid, but I'll pass the message on to the officer dealing with the case and have him call you back as soon as he can.'

More pacing, more waiting, more horrific visions in my mind… Jack was now fast asleep under a duvet on the sofa but Linda, who I'd thought had managed to get some sleep upstairs, had come down, having not slept a wink either.

I told her about the call and that they'd nothing new to tell me, and we waited anxiously in the dining room for the return call. When it hadn't come by 8am, though, I could bear to wait no longer, so I picked up the phone once again.

'I'm really sorry,' the same woman told me this time, 'but he's going to have to ring you later. He's just been called out on a Rapid Response.'

It was as if the world stopped in that instant. *Rapid Response.* I didn't know much about police work but the words felt like knives going through me. *Oh my God*, I thought. I knew what that meant.

I think I also knew at that point that they'd found her. Though I could hardly allow the thought to articulate in my head, it was as if my body knew. From my head to my feet I felt sick, overwhelmed by the words. *Rapid Response*. It was like a neon sign flashing in front of my eyes and it took a huge effort of will to stay on my feet.

Somehow I did so but within what felt like seconds, the call was disconnected and I put down the phone, feeling addled. I'd barely had the chance to formulate all the mass of questions that had started coming before I'd been rushed off the phone. At least, that's what it felt like – now my mind was all over the place.

By now, Jessica had arrived back at Linda's with Roger and Janet. She looked pale and drawn and I knew she was as fearful as I was, so I was anxious not to convey my terror to her. Before leaving with my brother the previous evening her last words to me had been question after question about Becca's possible whereabouts. 'What if she's hurt, Mam?' she'd asked me. 'What if she can't use her phone? What if she's lying somewhere, hidden by trees or a wall or something? What if she's badly hurt but no one can see her from the road?' Jess had a vivid imagination and was incredibly close to Becca so I knew that, when she told me that she couldn't feel her legs, it meant something bad – that she had this strong sense that something must be terribly wrong.

But I had to hold myself together for her, I must, and for Jack too. He was awake now and the first thing he said was, 'Is Becca home?'

'No, babes,' I told him, trying to keep my voice steady. But I could feel the panic inside me rising uncontrollably, even as I tried to steel myself. I felt like it was suffocating me and I knew I had to get out of the house.

'I can't stay here,' I told Linda. 'I just can't – I feel so helpless. I should be out there, I should be looking for her myself.'

'I know,' Linda agreed. 'It doesn't feel as if the police are doing much, does it? So why don't you and Roger do that? I'll stay here with Jack, in case the police call. That makes sense, doesn't it?'

I agreed that it did and so we could communicate with each other before we set off, I put some credit on Becca's iPhone. I was so grateful to have Linda at my side through all this. Her long experience as a midwife meant she was able to stay calm in a crisis and though I knew she was terrified too – she'd already admitted as much – her manner reassured me and helped calm me down. Hope, that was the thing: we had to hold on to hope.

We took Jess with us too. She was anxious to come anyway, plus she was the only one who really knew Aberkenfig and all the places Becca had mentioned to her the day before.

I could hardly function for fear now but, as we drove through the grey, lifeless Sunday-morning streets, I tried desperately to gather my thoughts and to think logically. It seemed sensible to follow the route I knew Becca had taken, so we eventually parked the car and began walking up Church Street, where I'd last spoken to her. It was the place where she was supposed to have been standing with Joshua Davies but apparently hadn't been. Which still made no sense.

'Go up here then?' Roger asked. I nodded and so we set off. As we walked, I explained the route Becca would have taken based on the conversations we'd had the previous afternoon. Now that we were there and I was describing Josh Davies's movements to my brother, it made even less sense to me than it had in the first place.

'So did he come from here?' he asked, pointing to where I'd already shown him was the area Josh lived.

'No,' I said, pointing in the other direction and trying to make sense of what was essentially senseless. 'He came up past the police station on the corner of his street, then crossed the road and went up the street where Daniel Ninnis lived. Then he cut across into Church Street and walked down the hill to where Becca was waiting. She was on the phone to me at the bottom when she saw him approaching.'

'Why would he do that?' my brother asked, as confused as I was. 'Why walk all the way round the top of Ninnis's street and round the road, when he could have walked straight up Church Street? It's double the distance.'

We were both agreeing it made no sense when we first heard the noise. It was a strange kind of noise to hear that early on a Sunday morning – like machinery of some sort; a pressure washer, maybe. The noise continued as we carried on up the road and stayed with us while we searched in silence. I was keen to knock on doors but we'd decided against doing that precisely because it *was* Sunday – a day of rest.

Which made the noise seem even more out of place – in both its duration and loudness. Perhaps more than one pressure washer, we decided. As we got closer it had been so loud that I decided it must have been several. But perhaps that was to be expected, I thought, trying to make sense of it. It wasn't actually *that* early, not by that time, so perhaps people were already out working on their gardens – the rest of the world going about its normal Sunday-morning business, while my own world had just become a living hell.

At the top of Church Street there was a small bridge that

spanned a narrow stream before continuing up to Park Road. We walked onto it, all of us with our hearts in our mouths, as we peered down into the slow-moving, shallow ribbon of water and scanned the earth beneath the bushes on the bank.

'Where to now?' my brother asked once we'd crossed it and seen nothing. 'Should we carry on up to the top?'

'What about Daniel Ninnis then?' Jess suggested. 'We could at least ask him, couldn't we? There's a chance he'll have heard something, even if he hasn't seen her.'

So that's what we did because although I knew Becca would never willingly spend time with him, Jess was right: there might be something he could tell us. So we turned our backs on the hill and woods – and all those strange machinery noises – with no way of knowing that, had we opted to go up there instead the source of those noises would have become immediately apparent and the search for my baby would have been over.

But our search was about to end anyway. We drew a blank at Dunraven Street, where Ninnis apparently lived, because although Jess knew he lived about halfway up the road, we didn't even know which side. So we decided that, rather than start knocking on doors to try and find him, we'd walk up to Sarn and Josh Humphreys' house instead. I still felt he might be key to Becca's disappearance or, at the very least, he had probably seen her at some point.

I felt torn. At the top of the hill there was a bank of tall trees marking the start of Pennsylvania Woods but Pandy Park, the place Becca had called me from the previous afternoon, lay in the other direction. Something kept calling me down there.

We started down the hill, all of us still looking carefully, trying to spot any place Becca might conceivably be partly hidden. At the end of Dunraven Street we crossed Bridgend Road. Passing Coronation Street next – the road Josh Davies lived on – we headed into Pandy Road and then into Pandy Park and into the same dismal tunnel Becca had walked through the day before.

Apart from calling Linda, which I did as soon as we'd entered Pandy Park, none of us spoke as we searched. We were all too consumed by fear, I think, to talk to each other so we just put one foot in front of the other, scanning the park.

I circled the building at the centre, trying to be methodical in what I was doing, and though I knew every corner we rounded might reveal her, blacked out, I was getting more scared of what I'd find with every passing minute.

I had just stopped by the building, unsure where to walk next, when I saw a lady across the park walking her dog. I suddenly remembered that Becca had mentioned something about seeing a woman with a dog when we'd been talking on the phone yesterday. I felt hope rise inside me – might this be the same lady? Would she know something? It seemed worth a try but, when we reached her, she had nothing to tell me.

'I'm so sorry,' she said, 'but I didn't take the dog out yesterday because of that big hail shower we had. I do hope you find her and bring her home safe.'

I showed her Becca's photo on the phone and she wished us good luck but, by now, I was beginning to wonder what to do next. Should we go up the hill to the woods or keep looking around the town?

We'd just emerged from the other end of the park when my brother's phone rang, causing my nerves to start jangling all over again. I so wanted it to ring but at the same time it was terrifying because ever since I'd heard those words 'Rapid Response', I knew there was a chance that, when the call came, it would be the one thing I most dreaded hearing in the world. I watched my brother carefully as he listened to whoever was speaking; studied his expression, his body language, every little nuance of what he did. And it was at that point that I think I really knew. It was as he disconnected that it hit me that I was soon going to be told exactly what I feared – the worst news a parent could *ever* hear.

'It's Linda,' he told me and his voice was strange. It scared me. 'She wants us to stop searching and come home.'

CHAPTER FOUR

THE WORST NEWS EVER

I knew immediately. I looked at my brother and I just knew. His face was grey.

'She wants us to come home,' he said again.

'It's bad news, isn't it?' I asked him. I was shouting, I realised. Frantic. On the verge of hysteria.

Jess was staring at me now, her expression blank and uncomprehending. She didn't realise what had happened, what *was* happening.

My brother had disconnected now, so I pulled the iPhone from my pocket and called Linda myself.

She answered immediately.

'What's happened?' I asked her. 'TELL me!'

'Come home, Son,' she said quietly. 'Just come home.'

Her tone confirmed what I already knew and, without even thinking about it, I grabbed Jessica's hand tightly, terrified of losing her too.

'Come on,' I said, yanking Jess's hand. 'We need to get home *now*!'

I tried to break into a run as we rushed back the way we'd just come but I found my legs kept on failing me, barely managing to support me. It was as if I was up to my waist in quicksand, being dragged down – sucked down.

Jessica, I kept on thinking, *I have to prepare Jessica*. I don't know why it was that thought, above all others, that kept demanding my attention but it did and, as we reached the car, I was trying desperately to think of how to tell her the thing I hadn't yet been told but didn't even need to hear.

'It's going to be bad,' I said as we got into the back of the car and my brother started the engine. I was shouting again, I realised. I didn't know why – I just couldn't seem not to. 'It's going to be the worst news ever,' I said and, even as I said it, I knew it was all coming out wrong. 'It's going to be bad, *very* bad: Becca's gone. She's not coming home.' It was burning in my brain, the thought of her being taken from me; of who'd murdered her. 'I will kill him,' I found myself saying, over and over.

Once again, my youngest daughter looked at me disbelievingly. Staring at me as if I was talking to her in a foreign language, she shook her head. 'No, Mam,' she kept telling me. 'She'll be OK. She's probably just in hospital or something. Or perhaps she's injured,' she suggested. 'She'll be OK, Mam – she'll just be injured.'

But I knew she was wrong. I didn't doubt that for an instant – that we'd get home to Linda and the police would be there and they would stand there and tell me my Becca was dead.

The journey – probably no more than ten minutes – seemed to take forever. As we swept past hedgerows and woodlands, I peered, sightless, at them, feeling a kind of shudder of complete dread passing through me. My brother didn't speak, just stared ahead and kept sighing, while Jess kept on saying it would be OK.

It wouldn't. That time had passed now. I believed that and it was terrifying. And with each passing minute I felt the hatred inside me rise for the monster who had done this to my child. If I'd been able to at that moment, I think I could have had the power inside me to kill them with my bare hands.

As we approached Linda's cul-de-sac, I saw Linda herself. She was in her car, driving Jack – presumably taking him to my brother Roger's house. And as we pulled up, I saw another car – a silver Ford Focus – parked outside. It had obviously arrived in a hurry, as one of the front wheels was half up on the pavement and I just knew it would be an unmarked police car.

The front door was open and my eldest brother Robert was standing there, his face grey. We followed him into the living room where, seated in the corner by the fireplace, was a police officer perhaps in his thirties, who Robert told us was DC John Doherty. He was apparently going to be our Family Liaison Officer, or FLO. The policeman's face confirmed everything I already now expected. The way he was looking slightly down, slightly off to one side, the way he held himself, the way he seemed to try and fix his face so carefully before raising his eyes and looking directly into mine.

'Sonia?' he began, speaking quietly.

Physically unable to speak, I nodded my head to confirm that he was addressing the right person. I watched everyone else sit down but remained in the doorway, transfixed, while the officer said those words that seemed to fill the whole room.

'Sonia,' he said again, 'we have found the body of a young girl who fits Becca's description, in a wooded area.'

I had known what he was about to say, more or less; I had been anticipating this moment. But as soon as the words left his mouth, an anger rose inside me, the like of which I had never in my life felt before.

Everything suddenly seemed to fall into place in that moment. There was this strange clarity, as all the puzzle pieces started falling into the correct slots, one by one. All the bits of information we did have, which now began to mean something different; all the horrible thoughts that had been in my head, now thoughts no more. They were facts. Someone had murdered my daughter. The words exploded out of me as shouts.

'Have you got whoever did this?' I yelled at the officer standing in front of me. 'Have you got the monster who did this? *Have you?*'

But he had no chance to answer because behind those words came a wave of nausea so powerful that I knew I was going to throw up. I ran to the downstairs toilet, yelling, '*No*!! Not my Becca!'

I was violently sick – more violently than I'd ever been before and, as I heaved, it was as if I was outside myself, feeling my body going numb. Bit by bit, I was shutting down. I'd not eaten in many hours – much less thought of showering or changing – yet my stomach couldn't seem to stop convulsing and trying to purge itself, as if desperate to rip out the pain.

What still seems incredible to me today is that emotions that are perhaps the most powerful a human being can ever feel are so impossible to adequately put into words. As my stomach finally stopped trying to turn itself inside out and the blood began pounding audibly in my temples, it was as if an overwhelming sense of dread had engulfed me. The unthinkable had already happened and the fear had now been replaced by a sense of darkness – a complete void, a closing in.

I felt alone in a way that was impossible to articulate; physically alone, even though the world and the people in it were so close at hand. Sound became muffled; I could no longer seem to make out what was being said to me – it was like in the films where they use camera trickery to zoom people away from you or suck you into a tunnel; a place where nothing seems real. I felt completely numb now. You could have stabbed me and I don't think I would have felt it. I couldn't compute, couldn't function. Couldn't quite make sense of what was happening. Kept repeating in my head the words John Doherty had said to me and, even though I'd known they were coming, it was like I'd had some sort of mental shutdown, as if my soul had been wrestled from within me. All my emotions and capacity for rational thought had temporarily stopped working. I was an empty shell that could only think one thing over and over: *What am I to do? What am I do? How am I going to deal with this?*

It was an intensity of emotion that no one could be prepared for. So how was I supposed to know how to begin to cope with it?

Though, to me, it had felt no more than a couple of minutes, they told me afterwards that I was in the cloakroom for ages. I spent most of it – however long it turned out to have been – fighting to regain a hold on my sanity. Trying to compose myself – desperate but at the same time determined – so that Jessica and Jack would have my strength to hang on to. *They mustn't see me like this*, I kept telling myself that, over and over. *I have to be strong for them now*. I left the downstairs loo, praying to God to let me *please* find that strength for them and, at the same time, praying that, actually, John the policeman wouldn't be there; that I had imagined it, that the whole thing was just an appalling nightmare.

But John Doherty was still sitting there, exactly where I'd left him, still waiting for me to finish what I'd started saying before I'd gone.

'Who, Sonia?' he asked me gently. 'Who are you talking about? Who do you want us to have got?'

I was shocked that he even needed to ask me. 'Well, it's obviously Josh Humphreys!' I shouted, the anger rising again like a beast inside me.

'Why do you think that, Sonia?' he continued. 'What are your reasons?'

'It's *got* to be him,' I managed to tell him. 'Becca saw him – she told me. And he wouldn't talk to us on the phone and wouldn't answer the door!'

'It's not him,' he said softly. 'We've already spoken to him, Sonia. We interviewed him this morning and he was in a club further up the valley last night – we've also spoken to people who've confirmed that. The reason he put the phone down on you was because he didn't know who it was and couldn't hear what you were saying due to the noise of the music.'

My head was all over the place now. Who had done this to Becca then? WHO? We'd phoned everyone Becca knew – well, everyone except for Daniel Ninnis because there'd be no point in doing that. He'd have been the last person she'd have been with. So who *could* it have been?

'Was it a stranger then?' I asked John Doherty. 'It must have been a stranger!'

All I could picture now was my dead baby. Where had they found her? And where was she now? I barked these questions at the policeman, my voice breaking as I did so. And all the while, Jessica was staring, uncomprehending, at both of us, asking if they'd actually checked her pulse and telling him to get her to hospital to see if they could save her.

'It's too late for that now, angel,' I kept repeating gently. But Jess couldn't seem to take it in. She just kept looking at me in disbelief, still thinking there was hope. 'What about the paramedics?' she asked John Doherty. 'Are they trying to save her?'

Watching and listening to my little girl, I felt my heart smash into even tinier pieces. How would my babies cope with this? How would they *ever*? How much pain could a human bear?

John, the police officer who'd had the horrible job of imparting the worst news any parent could ever hear to me, was in his thirties and, as I would find out much later, this was the first time he had ever had to do such a distressing thing, and the experience affected him deeply. But he was so kind and so professional, and so supportive that day.

I had heard only vaguely about Family Liaison Officers and all I knew I had gleaned from the TV. There's that phrase you hear, isn't there? 'Being comforted by Family Liaison Officers.' I'd never been sure what that meant but, like anyone else, I had an idea of police officers who stayed with a family 24/7, offering condolences and making cups of tea.

But this wasn't quite the reality. John's job as our Family Liaison Officer was to support us, of course, but this was as much about the investigation as anything. With our lives and emotions thrown into the worst place imaginable, his job was to build a relationship of trust, so that we wouldn't feel hurried, or pressured, or flustered. And that was because it was vital that we should be in the best place possible – under appallingly stressful circumstances – in order to help the police as best we could in their investigations.

A flustered, distressed witness forgets facts and muddles things and, as this was – as he gently explained – a murder investigation, it was now essential that we recall every tiny little detail. And remember it sooner rather than later, as time was of the essence. The more they established now, the better their chances of catching whoever did it. And that was something I wanted more than anything I had ever wanted – ever.

I had so many questions teeming in my head and was now desperate for answers. It was afternoon now – almost 24 hours since any of us had seen Becca and we didn't know a thing about what had happened after that.

The first thing John had to do, however, was take Jess and me home. On the way he explained that he would do his very best to help to answer any questions I might have – though on the understanding that he didn't actually have all the answers now, as the pathologist and forensics were still at the scene and they were still trying to piece it all together.

But there was something else he had to do; something I'd not yet considered. He had to go and break the news to Becca's father.

This really was something that had not even entered my

head. My relationship with my ex-husband, John, had been a fraught and, at times, frightening one, and finally finding the strength of mind to leave him at the beginning of the previous year had been one of the biggest and scariest things I'd ever had to do in my life. The time after that had been such a happy one for all of us. It had been such a difficult marriage, lived out in a house full of tension and unpleasantness, and the children seemed to be so much more settled and relaxed now it was just the four of us together.

It was to have been a new start for all of us and I knew I'd done the right thing when I believed I could see such a profound change in my children. They seemed to be the happiest I had ever seen them – so much more confident and outgoing – and I'd berated myself for not having had the courage to do it earlier.

Not that it had been an easy transition.

And now I had to face him with this. 'I want to come with you,' I said to John. 'It should be me that tells him.' I recall that clearly. That powerful sense it *must* be me who told my ex-husband that our daughter had been killed. I was overwhelmed by shock and grief and in the midst of it all I wanted him to feel the same hurt as I felt. I couldn't help it; I wanted to be there to see him suffer.

'I want to be there with you, Mam,' Jess said when John told us this, and I agreed.

I still felt the same sense of numbness and unreality as we drove to my ex-husband's flat and then approached the front door. I knocked and we waited for a response for some moments, Jess and I standing side by side with John Doherty close behind us – a reassuringly tall, towering presence.

My ex finally answered the door.

'Becca's dead!' I blurted out. And as John Doherty explained what he could, my ex-husband began crying and reached out to try and hug Jess, but she didn't want to know.

'We have to see each other again now,' he told her as I put my arm around her. Then he turned to me and what he said next will always stay with me.

'How could you let this happen, Son?' he said.

I didn't even furnish him with an answer.

CHAPTER FIVE

PURE EVIL

John brought us home at around noon. He offered to stay with us but I said no. I wanted him to go back to the police station and put all his energies into finding whoever had killed my beautiful child and then putting them behind bars, where they belonged.

'I'll be back at around two, though,' he told us, once I'd reassured him that Jess and I would be OK on our own. 'And I'll be bringing some other officers, from the Major Crimes Unit.'

He said the words gently but the reality was hitting home now. *Major Crimes Unit.* My daughter wasn't just gone; she was the victim of a 'major crime'. That meant a massive investigation beginning right in the middle of everything, which meant we couldn't even see her, let alone hold her. It hardly bore contemplating.

Jess and I clung to each other once he'd left, dazed and sobbing. We didn't know what to do with ourselves. We just stood by the back window, staring out, up at the mountain – a place where Becca often stood, just to admire the view. It was a beautiful place, our home in South Wales – a wild and wonderful place to spend a childhood. And with the mountain ever-present, watching over us.

It was while I was thinking that, half in a daze, when Jess suddenly jumped beside me.

'What?' I said. 'What is it, babes? What's wrong?'

'I heard Becca!' she said. 'I heard her voice, Mam – *so* clearly. She was saying, "Where am I?" Oh my God, Mam – what if she's lost?'

I turned to see her pretty, elfin face – they were so alike, Jess and Becca – and how wet it was. How pale. 'No, babes,' I said gently. 'She's in Heaven.'

Jess sobbed. 'But I heard her, Mam. As clear as if she was standing right behind me!'

I pulled her closer to me then and we stood there in silence, the tears streaming down both our faces.

I don't know how long we stayed like that – time appeared to have lost all meaning – but it seemed as if it was only moments later when Linda, Roger and his wife Janet were back with us – I'd asked them to come because my mind was in such turmoil that I was scared I wouldn't be able to take anything in, and trusted that they'd be clear-headed enough to ask all the questions I'd want answers to but might well forget to ask.

The police car drew up shortly after and I opened the door to John Doherty once again but this time there were three other officers with him. There was a young female officer who was to be a second FLO for us, Charmaine Kinson, together with two detectives: DS Paul Burke and DCI John Penhale.

They'd come from Bridgend Major Crimes Unit, they explained, once we'd assembled in my living room and they'd declined Linda's offer of cups of tea or coffee or cold drinks.

They offered condolences but I didn't want to listen to them. I didn't want sympathy – I just wanted my Becca back. But they weren't just there to offer me that anyway: they were conducting a murder investigation and they needed facts.

'Do you know a boy called Liam Thomas?' John Penhale, the Detective Inspector, asked. Beside him, Paul Burke, the Detective Superintendent, sat stiffly. He barely spoke throughout – just observed.

Liam Thomas was a name I knew, though I didn't know the boy himself. Not yet, anyway.

'I know he's a friend of Joshua Davies,' I told the DI. 'I remember Becca telling me he'd done work experience with Josh a few months back, in Aberkenfig primary school.'

'Do you know where he lives?' he asked then. 'Or which school he goes to?'

I shook my head. 'No, I don't,' I said. 'Was it him that did it, then? This Liam Thomas boy?'

The detectives both shook their heads.

'No, it wasn't him,' the DI said. 'Though we have made two arrests. We picked up two boys at nine-fifty this morning.'

I was stunned to hear this. Already they'd done that? My mind started reeling, it was so hard to take anything in. Two arrests – but who? Were they strangers? With a sickening jolt, I imagined my little girl having been bundled into a car and all kinds of horrific thoughts started running through my head.

'Who?' I wanted to know. '*Who* have you arrested? What are their names?' Do I know them?'

It seemed an age before the DS finally spoke and it occurred to me that he was waiting; gauging my reaction to what he was saying and what it might mean. He sat bolt upright, as if preparing for what he was about to tell me.

'Daniel Ninnis,' he said, causing me to gasp but also to start telling him that *did* make sense. I knew he hated Becca, after all. But before I could get a word out, he added, '...and Joshua Davies.'

I thought I must have misheard him. '*Josh*?' I said, conscious that all eyes in the room were on me. 'No,' I said, shaking my head. 'Not Josh, it can't be.'

But the DS looked right at me and nodded his head to confirm it.

If I'd been stunned before, now I was incredulous. The overwhelming feeling of nausea – that sense of dread that had been a constant in the pit of my stomach – seemed to intensify tenfold. I stared at the officer in shock and disbelief. Josh and Ninnis? It was *them*? It seemed inconceivable.

'Then it's Ninnis,' I said, trying to clear my head and think rationally. 'It *has* to be Ninnis. Josh would *never* hurt her, he just wouldn't. He always told me he'd protect Becca.' For all that I'd been cross with him, I was very clear on this. I even said it again: 'It can't be him, it has to be Ninnis.'

The DS shook his head. 'Actually, we think it was Josh,' he said gently. 'Though at the moment, they're both blaming each other.'

This, too, was impossible for me to comprehend but the police seemed so sure. They explained why too; explained that they had many, many years of experience of dealing with the most cold, vicious killers and that, in Davies, they had rarely seen anyone so cold and calm, particularly someone who was so young.

'I've not seen anything like it,' DCI John Penhale said. 'Not ever.' And the DS nodded in agreement.

Linda spoke then, surprising me, because I still couldn't take it in.

'He is just pure evil,' she said.

I could tell by her stunned tone that she was as shocked by this news as I was. She knew him well too; as I didn't drive, she had often given him lifts to and from our house over the years.

Both the senior officers nodded their heads in agreement. 'Yes,' the DS said, 'evil is the right word.'

That really hit me, that did – a senior police officer saying something like that. With everything he'd seen – all the bad people he'd come across over the years – to hear him saying that about Joshua Davies, well, it's impossible to put into words. All those years, all that time we'd welcomed him into our homes. I even remembered how, when his grades started dropping at school, Linda had suggested Becca should help him with his homework – he really had been that close to our family.

I needed to know then. I needed to know what the police knew – how it happened. What that monster had actually done to my daughter. I was reeling still, hardly able to think about it, pushing it away – trying to concentrate so hard on Jess and Jack, to hold things together for them. But now I could avoid thinking about it no longer, could avoid asking about it no longer: I needed them to tell me what he'd done to her.

It would be horrendous, I knew, hearing it, but at the same time I realised it might be easier knowing what they knew, what they'd found. So I had them tell me, which they did as delicately as they could. They told me about a head injury – that it was apparently a blow to her head that had killed her. About the evidence they'd so far gathered at the scene, which wasn't much yet, they explained, as forensics were still working there.

When they'd finished, it was as if I was communicating with them through a fog because what came to me was a picture – lots of pictures, actually – of all the times I'd seen murders reported on the TV. How, when they found a body, the police would cordon the scene off with coloured ribbon, erect floodlights and put a big tent up over the person to protect the evidence. My mind was racing now, visualising where Becca might be.

'Where is she now?' I heard myself ask them next and a part of me recoiled then because I didn't actually want to hear them say it – that she was 'still in situ' – it just sounded so horrible. 'They're still gathering evidence,' the DCI repeated gently and the way he said this confirmed it. She must be… She must still be lying there in the woods. My stomach seemed to shift, the nausea coming in a wave. I could feel something elemental begin to rise within me too at the thought of my baby child lying in the woods, all alone.

'You have to move her,' I said, trying to quell the awful image and keep my voice from breaking. 'I can't bear the thought of her lying there any longer. You have to move her *now*,' I repeated. 'And I have to *see* her. Please don't leave her alone there, I don't want her lying there another night alone. She's afraid of the dark. You *have* to move her!'

The officer explained that they would move her just as soon as they were able and that soon – tonight, probably – I would be able to see her. They just had to be as thorough as they could, collecting all the evidence before they did.

I understood this. And though desperate to see her, I was equally determined about them gathering that evidence, so they could put the monster behind bars for good.

But between then and now lay the next living nightmare. Jess now knew, obviously, but Jack didn't. As soon as they'd got the news, Linda had taken Jack back to Roger's house, so he wouldn't be there when we got back from our search and they had to break the news to me of Becca's death. And I was grateful for that.

But now I had to get him home from my brother's, where he'd been playing happily with his cousins, oblivious. With my heart in my mouth I called Roger to bring him home as soon as the police had all left, knowing I was going to have to tell him that his beautiful big sister was never coming home and that it was probably Josh Davies who'd killed her. How would he cope? How would any of us get over this? I dreaded the moment of him walking through the door.

Jess and I waited for him, both of us pacing as I'd done the night before, unseeing and silent except for repeating the same things over and over. 'How *could* he? He always protected her. How *could* he?' It was like a loop going round and round and round in our heads. And then there was my brother's car outside and there was Jack, and he jumped out so happy. Laughing and joking about all the fun things he'd done. And now I had to bring his happy world crashing down.

'Is Becca home?' were his first words on seeing me. He was even looking past me to see if he could see her behind me.

'I need to talk to you, babes,' I told him. 'Up in your room, OK?'

Even as we climbed the stairs, he was still full of his day and the things he'd been doing, even how he'd been helping to make cakes. And a kind of panic set in – did I have to tell him now? I didn't think I could do it. How could I ruin his life like that? Wouldn't it wait? Couldn't I leave it till tomorrow or the day after, or even the day after that?

But how could I? What if one of his friends told him? What if someone from the press turned up on the doorstep? And what would I tell him the next time the police arrived at the door? I had to tell him now – but how?

I sat down on his bed and had him come and sit next to me. He was beginning to look worried now, probably seeing the expression on my face. 'What's the matter, Mam?' he asked? 'Is Becca home yet?'

I felt like my heart was tearing in two. 'No, babe,' I said. 'She's not coming home again.'

'Oh, *nooo*!' he gasped, jumping off the bed and clutching a hand to his forehead. I got up too, and held him and coaxed him to sit back down with me. The look on his little face tore my heart to ribbons.

I held his hand tight. 'It's bad news, babes,' I told him.

'Oh, no, oh, no, she's not...' he began as we both started to cry.

'She's safe,' I whispered, 'in Heaven, with my mam and dad. They're looking after her now – till we can all be together again.'

I felt him twist beside me, to look at me. 'Who did it?' he demanded.

'Davies,' I said. 'The police think it was Davies who did it.' I couldn't bring myself to even utter his first name.

Jack jumped up. '*Josh*?' he asked me, wide-eyed with disbelief. '*Josh*? I will kill him, Mam! I swear to God I will kill him!'

Our FLOs, John and Charmaine, returned at around 7pm to take Linda and me to the Heath Hospital, in Cardiff. They had already advised me that it would be best if Jess and Jack didn't see Becca yet, as it would be so distressing for them. I realised they were right. Jack had already asked me endless questions about what had happened – what Davies had actually done to Becca – and it had been so hard trying to answer. How would he cope with actually seeing her lifeless body? How would Jess? It would be a nightmare that would haunt them forever, wouldn't it?

For myself, I was still praying – desperate to get there and see Becca for myself, but at the same time having this hope, even though I knew it was a forlorn one, that they would pull back a sheet and it wouldn't be her.

The journey was a long one – it takes around 30 minutes to drive in to Cardiff from where we lived – and to distract myself from how sick I was feeling, I asked question after question about what they'd found out so far, none of which they said they could answer.

By the time we arrived, I was in a daze – completely numb from the effects of the bitter cold. I think I was insulated by shock from my surroundings. Linda had worked at the University Hospital for years and I'd been there countless times but I had no sense of where I was or where I was being taken. It took all my mental energy just to put one foot in front of the other and I only went in the right direction because they were holding me and guiding my steps. If you'd stuck a knife in me at that moment, I don't think I would have felt it.

Once we got inside the hospital, Charmaine stayed with us while John Doherty went to let them know we were there. I don't recall anything being said; I think I stood there like a lost,

terrified child, almost incapable of any sort of communication.
All I could think of was what I was about to have to see.

When John came back, he took us to a busy waiting room just
off A and E, and then on to a small corridor that he explained
led to the room Becca was in.

'We'll just have to wait a couple of minutes,' he explained
gently, 'because Becca has a cut on her forehead that they're
going to cover up so that you don't have to be any more upset
than you already are.' He paused then. 'And there's one other
thing,' he went on, 'and it's that I'm afraid you won't be able to
touch her or kiss her. It's because of the forensic evidence – it's
really important that the evidence is preserved.'

He might have said more but if he did, I didn't take it in. All
this information kept coming at me and I just couldn't process
it – only that one dreadful fact that I couldn't get my head
around; that because of what had been done to my little girl, I
was to be denied the chance to kiss her goodbye.

I was speechless. But there was further distressing news to
come: John's next task was to let me and Linda know that my
ex – together with some members of his family – would be
going in to see Becca along with us.

I was stunned. How could that be right? It really upset me.
It felt like they were ghouls – why did they want to be there
now? They hadn't appeared to have wanted to see my Becca in
many years, most of them, so why now? It felt wrong; it felt
sick. I could only console myself with the knowledge that it
wouldn't be for long and that I'd be able to come back and say
a proper goodbye to Becca on my own.

John then went to check that they were ready but when he
returned and told us we could go in, it was if I was paralysed,

rooted to the spot. I was aware of Linda close by, to my right, and Charmaine just behind me, and aware of her gently nudging me to encourage me to walk into the room.

My mind was a seething mass of emotions. Part of me was saying, *Go on, go in – you never know, it might not be her*, but another part was frozen in fear, saying, *It is her, you know it's her*, and holding me back. I was so grateful to have my sister at my side, and felt her pain also – as a senior nurse, she had taken people into rooms just like this many, many times, having to hold them up, presumably, seeing their agony. And now she herself was having to do it, having to gaze upon the niece she loved so much, and she was being so strong for me. Without her, I know I would have collapsed.

I saw Becca's little face immediately and what scant hope I'd had was snatched from me. Though I took in the pure white sheet that covered her body, and the white material covering the rest of her head, it was her face that I kept my eyes on as Linda and I stood in the doorway, while it felt as if my heart was being torn physically from my body.

Linda began to edge me towards her, the silence now deafening, but then, without warning, it was shattered. There was a sudden commotion and a shout – a male shout – of 'I'm sorry, Bec!' and I remember being pushed and, to my shock and disgust, became aware that it was my ex-husband doing the pushing. He then barged past us and made a lunge towards Becca, his progress only halted by John Doherty's prompt action – he seemed to appear out of nowhere.

He held him back then, so Linda and I could go to Becca and watch her sleeping. There was a young lady standing there with her, just at the end of the bed, and I remember how very kind and gentle she looked and how much Becca would have approved of her looking after her.

My tiny perfect angel looked so beautiful – and also as if at peace. Even though there were bruises to her cheeks, her lips were curled up at the edges, which made her look as if she was just about to smile. With her head covered, I could only see a few strands of her hair and her tiny elfin ear.

I suddenly felt sick again then, seeing a trace of dried blood in it. How had they missed that? It's hard to describe quite how much that distressed me. My mind, which had calmed now I'd finally seen Becca, began racing all over again. I could hear voices too but couldn't make out what they were saying. I felt Linda nudge me and looked at her blankly, uncomprehending.

'It is Rebecca, isn't it?' she said, nudging me a second time, and I realised she was repeating what they needed to hear from me: my formal identification of my daughter. I could only nod but it was enough.

The job was done.

How to describe the pain of being a mother unable to kiss and touch her dead child? I so much wanted to put my arms around her, to kiss her, to physically soothe her, to hold her tiny hands. To put my lips against the rosy cheeks that, sitting against her perfect porcelain skin, had always made her look like a little doll.

She had been beautiful in life and she was beautiful in death. How could this be fair or right? Why my baby? I had given life and love to her and my job was to take care of her, protect her, so how could I bear to leave her here? She should be coming home with me.

Suddenly I became aware that we were expected to leave. 'I can see her again, can't I?' I asked. 'With Jess and Jack? They need to see her.'

'Yes, of course,' John said. 'Another time, maybe tomorrow.'

Reassured that we'd be back, I let Linda and Charmaine begin to lead me out then, still in shock, ill-prepared for what happened next – which was a barrage of questions from my ex's two sisters, who were now telling me how their brother really needed to see his other children, and bombarding me with questions and demands.

Linda stepped between us. 'This is not the time nor the place,' she told them firmly. She then looked across at John and Charmaine, who immediately stepped in. They told them to leave and escorted them all out.

I watched them all walk away, shell-shocked.

Jack, Jessica and I curled up together on the sofa that night. It would be the first night of many where we clung together, weeping. I couldn't bring myself to let either of them out of my sight and none of us could bear to be physically parted. Though sleep itself wouldn't come easily: every time I closed my eyes, that image of Becca lying on the hospital bed filled my vision. My whole head was too full of horrific thoughts and images and, when the tiredness overtook me, there was no respite either – I would just cry myself straight into another nightmare.

We went to bed eventually, all three of us crammed into my bed, with Becca's empty room a terrible presence just across the landing. The children actively fought sleep; they were much too terrified of the nightmares they'd surely have and lay either side of me, sobbing and dozing and waking again and sobbing, and there was nothing I could do to make it better.

At some point, however, we did all succumb to a deeper sleep because, when I woke in the early morning, it was with a jolt of sudden consciousness and with that came the thought that perhaps it wasn't real. Perhaps I'd dreamed everything; perhaps she was home.

Inching out carefully to avoid waking Jess and Jack, I crept into Becca's room, hoping in my half-asleep state to find her there as usual, sleeping in her bed, hands together as if in prayer, the way she so often slept – like an angel. But everything was just as she'd left it on Saturday lunchtime; the book she'd been reading the night before was sitting on the top of her bedside cabinet, her Rosary beads were hung up on her headboard as always and, as ever, she'd left the room neat and pretty. Her jewellery, her make-up, the clothes she'd chosen not to wear... all in the right places, all tidy.

On her bed, against her pillow, lay Angel. She was a teddy that Becca had bought from The Bear Factory a couple of years previously, and was wearing the outfit she'd bought the same day – a little white top with the word 'angel' embroidered on it, and little stars and flowers. How ironic that, of all the outfits Becca had bought for her since she'd got her, this should be the one she was in. I knew she'd have been cuddled up with her the last time she'd slept there, together with all her other favourite teddies.

She would never lay her head on that pillow again, ever. It was all real: it had happened, she was never coming home again. I picked up Angel, sat down on the empty bed and hugged her to me tight. When I started crying, I thought I'd never be able to stop.

CHAPTER SIX

A LIVING NIGHTMARE

My phone was switched on, as promised, at 7am on Monday.

It was the beginning of half-term week and we had made lots of plans, all of which rushed into my head as soon as I woke. I remembered the girls chattering away excitedly about all the things they were going to do. They'd planned a trip to the cinema and to the shops, both to window shop for clothes and to gather things they'd need for the party I'd told them they could put on for Halloween. We'd also planned to go as a family to the outdoor history museum in St Fagan's, on the edge of Cardiff, and, if it stayed dry, to perhaps even take a picnic.

My wretched thoughts were interrupted by the unexpected ringing of the phone and one of the first calls that came in was from John Doherty; he'd already explained the previous evening that today would be the day when Linda and I would need to go down to the police station and make our statements.

'How are you?' he wanted to know. 'Do you think you're up to it yet?'

I told him I'd like to get down there and do it sooner rather than later because the sooner I did it the less I'd be likely to forget, and I was fixated on recalling every tiny detail. I knew it might make the difference between getting a conviction or not. Things were starting to come back to me too, little details and oddities. Like the fact that, very early the previous morning, I'd had a text through from Joshua Davies on Becca's iPhone.

'Come home, Bec,' the text read. 'Everyone is worried about you.' He then went on to say something about her not being upset about the 'argument with Megan' – an argument that, as far as I knew, didn't exist. Having already set a trail that seemed to point to it being Josh Humphreys, was he then trying to set up another false trail; that she'd run away simply because of some row with her friend?

The content was one thing but it was *where* he'd sent the text that really struck me. He knew Becca didn't have her iPhone because he'd texted her on that number prior to their meeting and so, to me, it seemed clear what his motive might be; that sending a concerned text to her own phone would point to his knowing nothing about my phone because he wasn't there.

It became irrelevant shortly afterwards – just as soon as Liam Thomas's dad rang the police – but it was important to me because it was evidence of him scheming to get away with it.

So I was itching to get down there and set down everything I knew – as was Linda – even though I hated leaving Jack and Jessica. We were lucky, though – the children had, and still have, incredible friends and once I'd made them lunch, Ben, Jordan and Shannon arrived, leaving me to prepare for my trip to the police station. I wrote as much as I could remember of the events of the Saturday, as well as noting down the time and detail of every single phone call I'd made and received, as well as all the texts. I also made a note of usernames and passwords for Becca's social-media accounts, so that the police could access every detail of every online conversation, several of which, I could already see, would be incriminating.

John arrived to collect me at 3pm, as promised, and we drove down to the police station to meet Linda, who was going to drive herself. He explained that we would obviously need to make our statements separately: me with him, and Linda with Charmaine. 'And it might take a while, I'm afraid,' he added.

I had lived in Maesteg all my life but I'd never once been inside the police station. It had always just been there; a place I passed often but one I never imagined I would be entering. It was so much bigger than I'd imagined and, had John not been with me, I would have certainly got lost. I wasn't really taking in anything external anyway – all my thoughts were directed to the knowledge inside my head and how important it was that I didn't forget anything.

Linda arrived shortly afterwards and we were soon taken off – Linda with Charmaine, and me with John – to the rooms in which we'd both give our statements. Ours was a small grey room, featureless and functional. It had a desk with a computer on it and two wooden chairs – one at the desk, where John sat, and one to the side. It reminded me of the soundproofed audio rooms in the hospital where Becca had gone in to have hearing tests.

There were also the witness-statement sheets on which John would write my statement. We ran out of those very quickly.

John had been right – making my statement did seem to take forever. There were no prompts and no questions; all I had to do, he told me, was start at the beginning and simply tell him everything I remembered. So I began, trying not to forget a single thing, and it seemed that hardly any time had passed but somehow it was 5pm and Linda had finished her statement. She and Charmaine came and joined me for a coffee break, while John went out to deal with the press.

At this point, only our family and Becca's close friends knew anything but, when John returned, it was with the news that it was time to release Becca's name to the media.

'So we'll need a photograph,' he explained gently. 'Do you have one we could use, Sonia?'

This hit me with a jolt. It felt like such a horrible thing to have to do and I was anxious that we find one that Becca would have liked. Like any other teenage girl, she always wanted to look nice in photographs – although I'd sometimes tease her by putting baby photos up on Facebook, where we were friends, and she'd come right back with her usual comment of, 'Oh no, Mam!'

Everything seemed to be happening so fast but here was something I could do for her. I knew my choice of photo mattered a lot. 'I don't have any with me,' I told John. 'Can I get some from home for you once we're done?'

John went to ask the press officer who was waiting just outside the room. The press were the very last thing on my mind but they were obviously a big part of the process for the investigation because, when John came back in, he was shaking his head. 'I'm sorry,' he said, 'but they really need it as soon as possible.' He also explained that I couldn't go home in the middle of giving my statement, the first sheets of which, once I'd signed them, had already been whisked away so they could progress with their work – my information meant they could pinpoint key locations and enabled them to chase up CCTV and so on. And every minute, I knew, really counted.

'Maybe Linda could go?' I suggested. She had to get home anyway – she needed to have something to eat, being diabetic, and I was worried about her.

But it was a no-go. When they said 'as soon as possible', they meant 'right now'. 'How about choosing one on Facebook?' John suggested.

So I gave them the details and John logged in, and we sat there together while I tried to find a photograph I was happy for them to use. It was the first time I'd seen Becca's Facebook page since before the Saturday morning and before long I would find out that, had I looked at Davies's Facebook on the Saturday evening, I might have been able to work everything out for myself.

But it had never occurred to me to do that and it didn't occur to me now. All I could think of was how looking at Becca's page was a kind of torture, scrolling through pictures of her happy and smiling, and seeing all the silly jokes and bits of gossip on there. It was particularly difficult reading the things friends had posted on there over the last two days. 'Becca, please get in touch', 'please come home', 'text me', knowing not only that none would ever be answered but that these dear friends didn't even yet know why.

I chose one of Becca and Jack in the end and they did what

they needed to in order to retrieve it and process it, including cropping Jack out of it, which felt weird in itself. By now I was barely thinking straight and would so much have liked more time to choose but at that moment it was all I could do to make a choice for the waiting press officer – not consider how that photo would be beamed around the country before I'd even finished making my statement.

And once we were done, I could tell it had taken its toll on John, too. I didn't yet know him well, but I did know that he had children himself. One of his daughters was in school with Jessica, in fact, and going through Facebook with me must have affected him deeply. 'John,' I said as he got up to give the necessary information to the press officer, 'you will tell me exactly what happened, won't you?'

'*Everything?*' he said, standing there with his expression one of disbelief.

'Yes, everything,' I said. 'I need to know, even if you could just give me photocopies. I don't know when I'll have the mental strength to read it – and maybe I never will, but I need to know.'

I watched his eyes fill with tears then. Already he knew so much that I'm sure he wished he didn't about what had happened to my daughter.

Once we'd all had a coffee and Linda had left, John and I got back to work and, as I added to my statement, page by page, he began asking for clarification; he particularly wanted to know any tiny detail I could remember of any conversations Becca had had with either Davies, Ninnis or Thomas during the week leading up to her murder.

John was also keen to hear about the events of the Friday evening (exactly a year after the day of his and Becca's first ever date, as it happened), particularly the business of Becca deciding to change the arrangements and meet him on the Saturday instead. I had no idea why the change of date was so important to the investigation but by now I also understood that John couldn't tell me; I was a witness and, by law, I must know nothing at this point – because my being told anything by the police could jeopardise the case. Instead, I had to be satisfied with John's promise to me that, when the time came, the significance of those details would become crystal clear.

I felt that nothing in my head would ever be clear again by the time John had read everything back to me, made a few corrections and had me sign the statement. It was almost 9pm, though by now I had lost all track of time. I was just glad it was over with – except that, of course, it wasn't. Little did I know that over the coming months I'd be doing lots more of this.

In the short term, however, Jessica still needed to give her own statement (Jack was deemed too young), which John and Charmaine, who drove me home, were going to take her to do as soon as I got back. Hers would be done down the road in a place called Coity, near Bridgend, where there was a special interview suite for children.

They also reassured me that there would be no need for me to go with her and that the two of them would take care of her and keep her safe. 'And it's nothing like the room you've just been in,' Charmaine reassured me. 'It's designed to look like a normal home, with TVs and sofas and toys for the children to play with while they wait. She'll be fine. You stay at home and look after Jack.'

I was so grateful. I knew John and Charmaine would do just as they'd said and I was also anxious that it was late and that Jack needed me at home. It had been a long afternoon and, though their friends would have been a comfort and a distraction, I also knew that they wouldn't be able to properly vent their feelings till I was home, Jess was back and it was back to being just us.

Except that, when Jessica was returned to us at around midnight and we saw Charmaine and John out, I realised it would never just be the three of us. Becca was there too – for which I thanked God – her face swam before me constantly. I felt her with me as I went about all the chores that needed doing around the house on autopilot – made some food for Jessica, tidied up, took them both upstairs to sleep in my bed with me. And I felt her presence as I watched her brother and sister fall into an exhausted slumber, their faces finally peaceful, at least for a bit.

But there was another presence too and it was equally powerful. It was hatred like I'd never felt in my life. It was hatred that drove me now – making me constantly ask myself questions, mentally noting the answers, ready to pass on to John or Charmaine. The police had told me they were certain Joshua Davies had killed Becca and I believed them completely. I believed them even before the weight of evidence would begin stacking up so high, before finding out about all the damning things I had at this point still to be told. I believed them because it was all beginning to make sense to me too and I hated him more than I'd hated anything in my life. It spurred me on – I wanted him put away forever.

I didn't think I was capable of feeling things like that. I'd always been the kind of person who looked for the good in people, not the bad, but no more. I was almost glad not to sleep when we curled up that night. Because I knew that the worst pain of every single day from now on would be that moment when sleep changed to full consciousness and I'd remember. I hadn't dreamed any of it. It really *was* a living nightmare. My precious, precious daughter had been murdered.

It was in one of those half awake/half asleep moments that it hit me. I needed reassurance and answers that I could not get from the police, and I knew there was somewhere I might find both. I believe in God and that we will all be together again in heaven and I know – and knew then - that Becca believed that too.

We'd often talked about 'getting a message' to each other, and one of the things that I would say to her often was that if I died, I would always be her guardian angel, watching over her, Jack and Jessica, even in death. Never in a million years did I think that one of my children would cross over before me. So, in light of my religious beliefs, I decided to see a medium – to go for a reading to see if I could get a message from Becca.

I was desperate for any information – anything at all – and having read about other parents, such as Holly Wells's, and how they'd sought comfort from seeing a medium, I felt that I needed to do the same; it couldn't hurt, after all. I needed to know that there *was* something after we die; that my child was safe in the arms of God and that my parents were with her looking after her until I was reunited with her again.

There was a medium Becca and I knew of called Christopher Heath – in fact, back in the summer, she'd even asked me if we could go and see him the next time he was in our area. I called him and arranged to go and see him in his reading room, in the beautiful village of Llangynwyd.

I wasn't sure what to expect but I was surprised, even so, to see how beautiful and calming it was. There were fresh flowers arranged in beautiful vases, a statue of the sacred heart, various Rosary beads and crucifixes arranged around the room, and on the desk a bible, and I realised straight away, and gladly, that Christopher Heath was obviously a devout Catholic, just as we were.

The reading began with Chris asking for a personal item belonging to the person who had crossed over. I was wearing Rebecca's ring, one of her favourite rings, actually, and with some reluctance, I handed it over. For a few minutes he sat quietly holding the ring and then said, 'I have a gentleman here who crossed over with a heart attack.'

Was this my dad, I wondered? He seemed to describe him with such accuracy, before going on to say that he had a young girl with him. My heart skipped a beat. He said her name then, 'Rebecca'. 'Though I feel I want to be saying Becca, or Bec', he explained, going on to say that she was presenting to him in school uniform, and showing him how she'd crossed over.

I listened, rapt, as he described exactly where she'd been injured – and at a time when he couldn't have known anything about it, as it had yet to be reported in the press. How could he have known that?

He also told me she said that there were three people there that day, something he could have no way of knowing. Everything he told me was accurate, in fact, even down to the descriptions of the boys and the clothes they were wearing, the places where Becca had walked, including Pandy park, right down to the description of Pennsylvania woods.

Bec went on to talk about the things we had been doing at home since we'd lost her, and asked why I had put her photo in a big silver frame. I gasped at this; I'd put the picture in that particular frame just before leaving for the reading. I told her it was because I needed to have photos of her everywhere I went.

'I love you all,' she said, finally, 'and please, mam, don't cry. I'm fine now. I'm safe with Gran and Grandpa.'

CHAPTER SEVEN

MY LITTLE ANGEL

'Lil doll' – that's what I called Becca. I had done since she was a little girl. Because she'd always looked so like a little doll, right from when she was tiny. She had a mass of chocolate curls, which framed a perpetually smiling oval face, and those little cheeks of hers, they had always been so rosy – as if they'd been carefully painted on her by Geppetto. *My* little doll, she was, perfect in every way.

'Lil doll?' I recalled Joshua Davies saying, when he'd heard me calling Becca that one day. 'I love that,' he'd said to her. 'I'm going to call you that too.'

Although I'd said nothing at the time I'd been cross about him taking that name for my Bex. That was *my* name. And now he'd taken her from me as well.

From a very early age, Becca had always been busy. She was

born inquisitive and I knew, from well before she could even speak, that she was a bright girl, a girl who took everything in. So I would talk to her constantly and never use baby language either. Trains didn't become 'choo-choos' and horses weren't 'gee-gees' – she wanted to learn and I thought it made much more sense for her not to have to learn everything twice.

When she did start to talk, she barely stopped for breath. She chattered on endlessly and was wonderful company as well, always speaking so precisely and comically about anything and everything. I remember thinking how people would say being stuck with little ones could be boring but I never found that with Becca, not once: I loved being with her. I was as besotted as any new mother, I suppose, and found such joy in the simple things, like helping her to write her own name and reading her favourite stories to her at bedtime.

And she was so like a doll, both in her dress and demeanour. She loved dresses and frilly socks and for things to be matching, and would be at her happiest trying on things from my dressing-up box. And when Jess came along, she was even more in her element.

Rebecca took to school like a duck to water. Though I missed her terribly, I was so pleased to see how well she settled into the school community – so much so that one of the first things I remember during her first parents' evening was her teacher saying, 'I wish I had a full class of Rebecca's.' I felt so proud of my little angel then. And not only did she love to learn, she loved to be kind and to be helpful. She was always the one to make a beeline for anyone who was being bullied or was having problems – it was as if being kind was hard-wired into her soul.

She also loved to read, and read for pleasure every single day of her life, gobbling up books she liked the look of, even if they were beyond her at that point. 'But how will you be able to understand the story?' I'd ask her when she'd insist on borrowing a book from the library full of big, incomprehensible words. 'It'll be fine, Mam,' she'd say, with her usual faultless logic. 'If I get to a word I don't understand, I can ask you what it means, can't I? Then you can tell me and I can read on.'

So that was what we did, right through primary school and beyond. By the time she'd reached her teens, she'd already read several of the classics: *Jane Eyre*, *Pride and Prejudice* and of course, her namesake: *Rebecca*.

By the time Becca reached secondary school, she had already got her life mapped out. Her diaries were packed with optimism and ambition – full of her plans to do well at school, go to a top university, study law and then train as a barrister. But she wasn't just a career girl, she was a romantic as well and would spend lots of time planning every last detail of her wedding; drawing her ideal wedding dress, the bridesmaids' dresses too. Right down to the flowers she would have in her bouquet.

She was also a born 'little mum'. And being the eldest, she had two tailor-made little ones to mother. She would always want to help me feed and change them when they were babies and loved nothing better, once they were older, than dressing Jessica in pretty dresses ready for the outings we and Linda would often go on. Becca would also fuss around Jess when she got her clothes dirty – when it came to clothes, they were polar opposites – and soon became a second mum to Jack as well.

As they grew older, the girls became closer than ever and, once Jess started at high school, even more so. But because of the age gap between Becca and Jack, their relationship was different; she really always stayed as a second mum to him. When he was little, she'd sit and nurse him for hour upon hour and sing him to sleep when he was fractious. And as he got older and became anxious about one day going to big school, she would soothe and reassure him, telling him all about the comp and what fun he would have once he got there. 'And remember, when you start,' I heard her telling him, 'I'll still be in my last year, so you don't have to worry – I'll be there to look after you.'

Joshua Davies came into our lives in 2008 when Becca brought him home on the school bus for tea. He had blond spiky hair and a round baby face, which made him look younger than he was, even though he towered over her. Almost from the outset he was adored by everyone in our family; particularly Jack, for whom he was like a cherished big brother. Indeed he idolised him and would often ask if he could tag along whenever Becca and Joshua went to the park.

Davies was soon very much one of the family. I remember reading messages from that time between Joshua and Becca in which Bec was teasing him about how he was so protective of Jack. 'I would be,' he responded, 'because I treat him as if he was my own son. I love him to bits and even worry he'll get hurt playing on his skateboard.'

It was as if, little by little, he was becoming a real part of our family; something he always seemed very keen to be. Every time he came round, we'd talk for hours about anything and everything – and particularly music because, unusually for a boy of his age, he seemed to like all the same oldies I did. His relationship with me seemed a particularly big thing to him. 'Becca,' he'd say, 'you know you could never have another boyfriend, don't you? Because your mother will always like me the best.'

And, oddly, this continued long after he'd finished with her. Constant questioning and badgering, even when she first met Josh Humphreys, which made no sense, given that Davies had been the one to end their relationship. But that didn't seem to make any difference. They'd still have conversations in school about it. 'Does your mother like him?' he would want to know. 'I bet she prefers me to be your boyfriend.' And when she told him that, yes, I *did* like Josh Humphreys, he would go away angry and in a huff.

But even before he finished with Becca, I had begun to see another side to him. Like any teenager, he would test the boundaries and, perhaps because he felt so comfortable in our home by this time, he seemed less and less concerned about where he did it too. He could never sit still for five minutes and, on one particular occasion, was jumping around with a foam bat and wand (toys of Jack's) when suddenly he came out with a shocking pronouncement: 'There's this guy living here in Maesteg who is in the Ku Klux Klan,' he told us. 'I want to join them as well – we all should.' We looked at him aghast but he didn't seem fazed by it. 'We should all join and hunt the blacks and hang them all from the trees,' he continued.

'*Josh!*' said Becca immediately. 'Don't say that, that's racist!'

I was still looking at him at that point, wondering if I'd heard right, when he added, 'Do you know him? I'm serious. I'm sick of them – they're taking over our country!'

'No, we don't know him,' I said sternly. 'And we don't *want* to, we're not racists. Josh, don't say things like that – you don't mean it.'

'Yes, I do,' he said and then started playing with the bat and wand again, jumping round the room, jabbing his 'weapons' in the air, saying, 'Hang the pakis! Get rid of the blacks!'

And by the look of it, he meant every word.

Both of us were mortified but particularly Becca. It was a side to him she hadn't seen before and she confided in me how much it had upset her. They'd argued later and she told me how shocked she'd been to hear him ranting on about killing innocent people.

I, too, was beginning to see a change in him, thinking how each time I saw him how much he was changing from the baby-faced boy I'd met a year and a half before. I was also concerned about the kinds of things he and his friend Daniel Ninnis got up to. They'd regularly go up to the forest for hours, doing goodness knows what, and sometimes even camp there overnight. And sometimes they'd ask the girls from school to go with them.

'Don't you ever go there with any of them,' I remember warning Becca. 'Never go anywhere so out of the way with a bunch of boys, ever. Even if there are lots of girls going, it's not the place to go. Always stay where there are shops and plenty of people around.' It was like my mantra.

But Becca would always be so quick to reassure me. 'Don't worry,' she'd say, laughing. 'Why would I want to go anywhere near a dirty, muddy forest and mess up my clothes and get mud all over my shoes? No way in the world would I go up there!' she'd insist and I believed her. She loved her clothes and her shoes and always kept everything so nice, particularly when it was new and especially precious.

And Becca had been wearing very precious clothes that day. Her high-heeled boots, her best jeans and her brand-new

Superdry hoodie. So when the police had told me where they'd found her just two mornings earlier, I knew one thing as surely as if I'd been there myself: that she did not go up into that forest willingly.

I didn't know which was worse. Being asleep and having nightmares or lying awake, remembering. Because remembering all that had gone before – knowing that was it, her life was over – was like a living nightmare in itself. In any event, by Tuesday morning I felt as if I was walking through a dark fog. And through the fog came the sound of the phone ringing. It was John Doherty, to ask me if he could have Becca's latest diary as a matter of urgency, though he was unable to tell me any more than that.

As we'd moved so recently, it was a real struggle to find it. I searched high and low but it was nowhere to be found in Becca's room and I wondered if, perhaps, she'd got rid of it for some reason – although that seemed completely out of character. It was in the small hours that it finally hit me that it might not even be there – it might be among the stuff that was still at our old house. We'd moved most of our belongings but hadn't quite finished and still had a few things left to move.

The next day I went round and straight up to Becca's old bedroom, which was empty, though she did have a cupboard set high on one wall. I found a chair and climbed up to look in it. Almost straight away, I saw them: a pile of five diaries, including the most recent, but something else too – things she'd written on the back of the cupboard wall. There were drawings she'd done of the two of them, and also his name, in big swirly letters surrounded by love hearts.

I got my phone out and took some photos, as I felt sure John would want to see these and, as I got down, I noticed something else as well. Becca's walls were bare now as we'd taken her posters down and, as I looked around me, I realised something I'd not noticed before. That someone – and I didn't doubt for a second that it was Davies – had written things like 'Becca is a slag' directly onto the walls in coloured hairspray. I could see where Becca had tried to clean it up before covering it all with posters.

I called John – pointing out that I knew decorators were due in and that, if they wanted to see it all, they would need to come quickly. He and Charmaine met me there the following day and took photos themselves. By which time it had begun to sink in. What sort of mind games had that monster been playing with my child? I'd handed over the diaries and, true to my word to Becca, I hadn't looked at any of them. And now I could no longer bear to.

In the midst of all this, we had another, more formal meeting. On the Tuesday, John and Charmaine brought the Superintendent round, plus a couple of other officers I'd not met before. There were four of them, all gathered on the doorstep with serious expressions, some in uniform, others not – the FLOs, the DS and the DCI as well, so many different letters to remember.

As soon as I'd known they were on the way, I had called Linda and asked if she and our brother Roger and his wife Janet could come up and join us. I knew I wasn't thinking straight but had found enough presence of mind to have them with me, so they could listen to what the police said as well as me; I felt sure there would be loads I'd forget. They could also ask questions on my behalf as they thought of them – again, I knew I might not think straight enough to do so myself.

Because I didn't want them to be distressed any more than they already were, I sent Jack and Jessica upstairs to play on their DS consoles and showed the policemen into the living room. It was a squash but eventually everyone had found somewhere to sit, bar John Doherty, who took up a position near the door. He was already becoming a reassuring and calming presence.

The key police officers introduced themselves politely, all lined up in a row on the sofa, and then the Superintendent looked at me with a solemn expression. 'I would like to offer our sincere condolences,' he said quietly, 'to both you and your family at this sad time.'

I had come to fear this sort of thing already. Any hint of commiseration, of kindness, especially now, seeing the sadness in his eyes, was like a red rag to a bull to me. Not because it angered me but because it frightened me – as soon as anyone said anything like that to me, my reaction was immediate – I would find it almost impossible to stop myself breaking down. But it was important I did so. I knew I had a lifetime of crying ahead of me and right now I must stay strong and focused for Becca. I was still in shock – I don't think I'd quite got my head around the fact that I would never see her again – so I didn't want to hear it in any case.

'What's happening?' I blurted out, interrupting him. 'What have you found out?'

The Superintendent spoke calmly and precisely. 'As you know,' he said, 'both the boys have been blaming each other…'

I nodded. 'But we have decided to charge Joshua Davies with her murder.'

He paused then and we all let out a sigh of relief: they were going ahead. *They must have enough evidence*, I thought. *Good.* 'And Ninnis?' I asked. 'Has he been charged too?'

The Superintendent shook his head. 'No,' he said. 'We released him this morning without charge.'

I was horrified, because at the time I thought he must be as much to blame as Davies. '*What?*' I said, 'surely not? Surely you can't have let him go?'

The DCI spoke then. 'All the evidence is pointing towards Davies,' he explained. 'And, as of now, we're satisfied that he was acting alone. But we're still waiting on the results of more forensic tests,' he went on. 'It's a fast-paced investigation and there is a lot of evidence still to be gone through but, at the moment, it all points towards Davies, as the Superintendent says.'

Which reassured me a little, even though it felt all wrong to me that Ninnis was free.

That evening, I was asked to return to Maesteg Police Station, this time for a meeting with the Assistant Chief Constable, Matt Jukes. He had called the meeting so that he could introduce himself and explain to us all in person how they planned to progress with the investigation, and hopefully answer as many as he could of our endless questions.

Once again, I asked Linda to go with me (the rest of the family travelled separately) while Roger stayed at home to look after Jessica and Jack. Though I didn't only need Linda to ask the questions and make notes. It was also because my ex-husband John was going to be there and I knew the atmosphere would be tense.

For most people who've come out of a difficult relationship, the sensible thing – and the thing that I'd done up to that point – would be to keep away from their ex as much as possible. Sadly, for me, this was no longer possible as my former husband and I had been suddenly thrown together, and in the worst possible circumstances imaginable.

I was dreading having to see him again, particularly in my current vulnerable state, and I needed Linda with me as much for moral support as anything. She'd protect me from him, I knew.

He had come with relatives too. As we were shown into the police-station conference room and Linda sat me down in the centre of my family, I could see that he'd brought his two sisters as before, as well as two of his nieces. I didn't understand that at all. Was this really the place for such young women? It also felt wrong that people who didn't know Becca nearly as well as we did should have the right to be there as well.

But the meeting wasn't long. The Assistant Chief Constable introduced himself and, like the Superintendent before him, expressed his condolences and reassured us that he was overseeing everything. He told us they would do everything in their power to investigate Becca's murder thoroughly and keep us informed of progress at all times throughout.

Then it came to questions and, straight away, I decided that, although I had many, I didn't want to discuss them in front of 'relatives' who were essentially strangers. I would ask John, I decided, once the meeting was over. So instead, I just sat there and listened while my ex-husband asked *his* questions – questions that, to me at least, were mostly irrelevant – he'd never even known any of the boys involved – or to which I already knew the answers.

We did find out a couple of key things, however. Although the officer made it clear that, as key witnesses, there was much Linda and I *mustn't* know yet, he was able to tell us the course of events that led to Davies's and Ninnis's arrest. Liam Thomas had apparently told his mother on the Sunday of his suspicions about what Joshua Davies might have done to Becca. It had been his father who had then called the police. But for the moment, we had to accept that they could tell us very little more about anything, for fear of jeopardising their hope of a conviction.

This was very much on my mind as we finally filed out of the police station but, as ever, my ex seemed more interested in getting to me. He marched straight over to me as Linda was helping me to the car park, wanting to know when he could see Jack and Jess. I could barely think straight, let alone speak to him – had it really not sunk in with him? My little girl had just been murdered. Just three days ago! And her brother and sister were, like me, reeling. Did he really think I'd want to discuss things like that with him right at that moment?

Linda grabbed my arm and led me away and I was so grateful. Because the last thing on my mind was that man I used to be married to. My mind was much more focused on Davies, And whatever evil plot he had hatched to end her life. And there was one question I knew I wouldn't have answered for a long time.

Why did he do this evil thing to my daughter? WHY?

CHAPTER EIGHT

HIGH HOPES

John Doherty called me on the Tuesday evening to tell me that Joshua Davies would be appearing before Bridgend Magistrates Court the following morning: Wednesday, 27 October. I was still reeling from what I'd learned about only Davies being charged.

'Why just him?' I asked John. 'Why not all three of those boys?'

He was patient, explaining that it was Davies alone who was being charged with Becca's murder, which meant he was the one who was going to trial. It was frustrating at the time because, without the facts of the case, I didn't know that it was just Davies who had done this, even if the other two were with him on that day. At the time I was equally angry with all of them, whatever the police were telling me.

As ever, John couldn't give me any answers to the questions that were teeming in my mind. It was frustrating but there was nothing to be done about it and, conscious of what a good man he was and how much he and Charmaine were supporting me, I didn't press it. I would find out in the end.

'Should I go to court?' I asked him. A part of me was desperate to physically see Davies – to look into his eyes and transmit the hatred I felt for him. But another part was anxious about leaving Jack and Jessica, and for what? Would it help? Would it change anything?

'I wouldn't go unless you really feel you must,' John counselled, 'because it'll be very quick – over in no time at all. He'll only be in the dock for a few minutes, no more – just long enough to confirm his identity and date of birth and so that the case can be formally referred to Crown Court. They'll take him straight back into custody after that,' he finished.

Back... Back to where? Where exactly were they keeping Davies? I hoped it was a horrible place. He had ended my daughter's life and a hole in the ground would have been too good for him: he deserved to be in hell.

Even after putting the phone down, I still dithered about going to court. I so badly wanted to see him – in truth, I wanted to physically attack him – and John, perhaps sensing that I might change my mind, even called me again first thing on the Wednesday morning to double-check my plans. But although I was torn, I had to balance my need for vengeance with my fears for my other two children. They needed me with them and strong for them, so I focused on mothering them. The time for answers, for seeing that monster in the dock, would come, I knew. In the meantime, I had to keep my focus on my family and how we were going to get through each new day in the new house that had represented so much hope and happiness for us all.

Nine days earlier, that was all. Just nine days ago we'd moved in.

It had all been a rush too, moving out of our last house. Our landlord was moving abroad and selling all his properties, which meant we had to move out with very little time to get organised. But, thanks mostly to Becca, we were. The removal van had been booked for the Friday but, as we already had the keys (Becca being Becca – i.e. organised to a fault), she had been badgering me to let us move some of our stuff in on the Thursday, 'just to start getting everything arranged'.

She was a great planner and, true to form, had planned the move to perfection, so it was great to see her looking well and happy. She'd been off school that week, following another bout of nausea and blackouts, and the fact that the consultants hadn't managed to get to the bottom of it was a constant anxiety in my mind. But right now, she was healthy and feeling good so I was grateful. We'd get to the reason eventually, I reassured myself, having no idea that events to come would overtake that whole issue and, at the same time, provide a possible answer to the mystery.

When Friday came, we had a plan (also decided upon by Becca). I would oversee the moving out, back at our old house, while she would be in the new house, ready for the removal van, so that she could direct them about where everything needed to go.

The house was already spick and span and ready for us. Having had the keys earlier in the week, I'd spent a busy few days with my brother Robert and Becca painting everything brilliant white, rather than magnolia, as we'd all agreed that it would provide a brighter, better background for all the bright canvas paintings we'd amassed over the last couple of years, as well as our enormous family photo gallery.

Our last house had been in the beautiful village of Llangynwyd, close to Maesteg, and we'd lived there since early 2009. It had been our first family home since I finally left my husband and, free to start our new lives together, we loved it.

Llangynwyd was steeped in Welsh history and we soon immersed ourselves in all the stories and traditions. It even had its very own tragic love story, in the shape of the *Maid of Cefn Ydfa* – a young girl called Ann Thomas, who was forced to marry into the wealthy Maddocks family against her wishes, her true love being a local boy called Wil Hopcyn. Unable to be with her, a broken-hearted Wil then left the area and, though Ann went through with the marriage, it's said that she pined so much for Wil that she soon became seriously ill. Close to death, she called for him and he hurried to her bedside, where she died in his arms, aged just 23.

Always a romantic, Becca was greatly moved by the story and in the summer, just a few short weeks before we lost her, she'd insisted on going up to see Ann Thomas's grave. It was part of a school project and she was determined to see it for herself though, as she'd been suffering from one of her bouts of inexplicable weakness at the time, she'd struggled to make it up there. The site was very steep and she'd had to hang onto my arm, struggling for breath.

Still, she was so pleased to see it, and was full of it on the way back down. It was just the sort of love story she loved the best.

The other great village tradition was the *Mari Lwyd*. This was a midwinter tradition, which ran from December through till January, in which a visiting wassail (a group of travelling singers) would go from house to house, accompanied by a person dressed as a grey horse (the translation of the Welsh *Mari Lwyd*) in the hope of gaining admittance, food and drink. Becca loved being a part of it, as did all of us. It was a wonderful way to get to know all our neighbours that first Christmas, particularly our close neighbours and friends Clem and Zelda, two lovely, lovely people with a grandson Jack's age, who became – and still are – such good friends.

Though it was hard to leave, I was consoled that we wouldn't be far away and, with the new house being so much closer to my family, we were all very excited about our future. And, as it turned out, Becca had already been thinking about hers.

The old house cleared, Linda and I drove the short distance to the new one, where Becca was already getting stuck in. She'd taken charge of labelling all the boxes over the previous couple of weeks and so when I arrived, I expected everything to have been put into the room it was allocated to. And this was the case, at least downstairs, but when I went upstairs, it was to find all my boxes stacked up in the biggest bedroom and Becca busy in the smallest one, unpacking. I was confused – why had that happened?

In our previous house, I'd decided to give Becca the biggest bedroom, as she had so much more stuff than me. I didn't need masses of space, whereas she needed the storage for all her books and clothes and shoes. It also made sense because Jess's bedroom was adjoining, through double doors between them – even though the pair of them would more often than not sneak into one or the other's rooms after I'd sent them both to bed and told them to go to sleep.

'Why are your things in here, love?' I asked her. 'This was going to be my room.'

She shook her head and paused in her unpacking. 'I changed my mind,' she said firmly. 'I thought I'd have this one instead, if that's all right?'

'But I want *you* to have the big one, love,' I said. 'I don't need all that space.'

But her mouth had a determined set to it. 'No, it makes much more sense for you to have it, Mam. I'm not going to be here that much longer, am I?'

This took me aback. 'What on earth d'you mean?' I said, horrified.

She must have seen the shocked look on my face because she grinned back at me. 'Mum, I'm talking about *university*! After all, it's only going to be three years now, isn't it?'

Even though I knew how much it meant to her, and how proud and thrilled I'd be for her, I didn't want to think about her leaving us just yet and said so. She grinned again then and hugged me but still refused to change rooms.

Little did I know we'd only have her for nine more days.

We hadn't been in our new home long but Becca, being the kind of girl she was, had already stamped her personality on the place.

As Wednesday became Thursday – the concept of a 'day' had lost all meaning – I felt Becca's presence all around me. I kept getting flashbacks to that morning, remembering how happy and hopeful she had been, seeing her moving about the house, singing in the bath, trying on clothes. I couldn't seem to stop myself focusing on every tiny detail of it – what she'd worn, what she'd said, how she'd hummed to herself as she got ready. And with those flashbacks came others – of where her body lay now, in the hospital; of that Spartan, clinical room, devoid of any warmth or comfort. It felt all wrong – she should have been at home with us, home where she belonged, with her family. It didn't matter that she was gone – the thought of her physical body lying there all alone was intolerable. And as soon as that image came into my head, I had to force it away, to try and shut part of myself down before I went mad from the pain.

But there was no escape. I couldn't stop torturing myself with thoughts of the future either. A future without my daughter, who had such grand plans for her career, which I'd always known she would achieve. Thoughts of her excitement about going to university, getting her law degree, starting her career – how did we go on now? How did my other children pull their shattered lives together without the constant of their older sister's caring, loving, guiding presence? I thought of Jess, who'd known nothing of life without Becca – her best friend, her mentor, her irreplaceable big sis. And I thought of little Jack, for whom Becca was another little Mum. How would they ever get *their* lives back on track? How could they even go back to school again?

If the thought of the children going back to school was difficult from the point of view of their pain, there was another consideration, particularly for Jessica. She attended the same school as Becca had. The same school that Daniel Ninnis and Liam Thomas attended; two murderer's buddies, whom she might now have to face every day.

Once again, John was patient but firm. I was a witness, which meant they had to be very careful about what they told me. If they put a foot wrong, they would jeopardise the chance of getting a conviction because they would give the defence lawyers the grounds to claim there'd been a mistrial.

'I'm sorry,' John told me, 'But all I can tell you is that all the forensic evidence was gathered and presented to the CPS (the Crown Prosecution Service) and, on the basis of that, it was decided to charge Davies alone and to make the other two boys witnesses for the prosecution.'

Which meant there was no choice but for Jess to have to face them, however traumatic that was going to be for her. It was bad enough that she would have to deal with the other members of the Davies family – his brother Jordan, who was in her year, and the lad who his grandmother brought up, Tyler Harry (who I thought was his half-brother). I had thought about all that already and how hard it would be. And now this as well – that she would have to go to school every day and see Liam Thomas and Daniel Ninnis. How fair could it be that Jessica had to attend school with the two boys who were with her sister's killer on the day he committed her murder?

It was just as well that I didn't know then what I would find out in the coming months, as I might not have been responsible for my actions.

CHAPTER NINE

KEEPSAKES AND DIARIES

Now that Davies had been formally charged, it was the police's job to build a case against him and to that end they needed every shred of new information they could get. The next few days, therefore, became an endless round of questions.

John and Charmaine were in constant contact with us still. One of them would telephone me every morning anyway, just to check if we were OK and to see if we needed anything. But they would also now phone me at odd times of the day and come round to the house regularly and try to tease out tiny new details. Of course each one of those new bits of information they were gathering would mean I would have to make a new statement. By the time they finished getting new facts from me, I think we were up to about version 14!

But it was of crucial importance that they left no stone unturned because they would be up against a rigorous defence team. So they impressed upon me that they wanted to know every last thing about Becca, whether it seemed relevant to me and Linda or otherwise – what she liked, what she disliked, who her friends were, how she spent her time, even down to what she mostly liked to read.

A couple of weeks after Becca's death, Charmaine, our second FLO, came over and asked if I'd take her up to Becca's bedroom and show her some of her books. Which I knew wouldn't be easy – although I never knew quite how it would affect me because going there had become strange emotional territory. At times it was a comfort, yes, because sometimes I felt a powerful need to feel more physically close to her, but at other times it was a torture to so much as pass the bedroom door.

'I know how hard this is going to be for you,' Charmaine said, as I led her upstairs and into the room that day. Having her with me and going in there with a clearly defined purpose was actually a big help though, and we were able to sit down together on Becca's bed.

I had left everything pretty much exactly as she had left it; even lining all her shoes up along the wall because I knew that was what she'd have done – doing so made me feel closer to her. It was probably also of benefit to the police that I hadn't moved anything around. After all there was almost certainly evidence here – evidence that could help them.

'May I?' Charmaine said, pointing to the books on the bedside table, of which there were two, as was usual for Becca. The first was Anne Frank's *Diary of a Young Girl*. 'I remember reading this in school,' Charmaine said, 'such an incredible story.'

I nodded. 'She's read it several times,' I said, as she picked it up and looked at it. I was struggling to keep my composure.

'Ah, and a *Twilight* book,' said Charmaine, picking up the other one.

'All the girls like these books,' I told her. 'And the films.'

'I know,' she said. 'They're incredible popular, aren't they? Are they good?'

'I don't know,' I admitted. 'I've never read one or seen one but I almost feel I know them because the girls have told me so much about them. Maybe I should now, see what all the fuss is about.'

It was comforting to sit and talk to Charmaine. I told her how much Becca had always loved reading – and writing too. She'd done a lot of that as well. I told Charmaine how Becca had shown me several of her stories over the years and how descriptive they were becoming, especially what she called her 'dream' stories. I told her how Becca had always had an incredible imagination and how I knew that, if she had put her mind to it, she might one day have had stories published as well. And, in the midst of all the pain, I felt glad that Charmaine was there, that we'd been allocated a police officer I could talk to.

But as well as insights into what sort of a girl Becca was, the police also needed cold, hard, incriminating evidence. Which meant they had to take Becca's laptop, loathe as I was to say goodbye to it, and they needed to take Jessica's as well.

'There might be something of use to us on them,' Charmaine explained, 'what with Davies having spent so much time at your old house – teenagers are always going on one another's computers, aren't they?'

And she was right, he'd been round loads – at one point he'd been almost like a lodger – and he had definitely used both girls' laptops (I even had a photo of him on one). I also remembered that he'd one day taken over both their computers using something called 'remote assistant' on his iPhone.

Both John and Charmaine were excited to hear that. And although, again, they couldn't tell me anything about what was going on, I could only hope that he'd incriminated himself in some way and that my own 'remote assistance' might prove to be his undoing.

It was the need for physical evidence that probably hit me hardest. Letting go of Becca's laptop was one thing, but having to let go of things that felt a part of her physical presence in our home was another thing altogether. I understood the need for the police to scour her bedroom for evidence – and, of course, I wanted them to find anything that might help prove Davies's guilt. It was still horrible even though they assured me I would get everything back again, because I wanted to hang onto every little part of her.

Already Jack and I had carefully gathered some strands of her hair from her pillow and put them safely away in a little box because I didn't know if the police would even let me have a lock of her hair. We'd also managed to find a couple of her beautiful long eyelashes, so we tucked them away safely as well.

But it had to be done – it was apparently a vital part of the process, as Charmaine always pointed out to me so gently. I was so grateful to have someone like her by my side through that gruelling period. And I was also constantly astounded by her professionalism. She was a striking young woman; over 6ft tall, with long blonde hair that was always tied back in a neat ponytail and with a real presence about her – very useful for a policewoman – and a strong sense of justice and right and wrong.

Ever since she'd made that comment about Davies while we'd been waiting to see Becca in the hospital, I knew she knew all sorts of things that she couldn't tell us; things that, like John, she'd probably rather wish she didn't know. But her strength was amazing, as was her commitment to her job. She worked tirelessly, for such long hours, and never seemed to take a break. Often, I would think of something late in the evening and even when I called her after midnight – she had always told me to call the minute I thought of something, whatever the hour – she would be in the same place, it seemed: the incident room at the Major Crimes Unit.

It had been Charmaine who'd reassured me that Becca wouldn't have suffered. That from her injuries, they knew she would have died very quickly, which was a shred of comfort that I really clung on to. And there was something else too – her total confidence that we would bring Becca's murderer to justice. So, distressing though it was, as her room had become such a shrine to us, I knew I had to let John and Charmaine take away so many of her personal things.

So they took Becca's perfume and various items of jewellery and asked me to show them the make-up I thought she'd probably put on that day. They also wanted her two make-up bags, in which she always neatly tidied away her cosmetics; the big burgundy vanity case that she kept most of it in and the smaller, floral one she took with her in her school bag every day, or if she was going out anywhere. That both were there in her bedroom instead of on her person was another reminder of the wicked brutality of Davies's plan. She had skipped off to meet him, secure in the knowledge that she would be back home – and with him in tow – in a couple of hours.

One item in particular was apparently crucial to the investigation: they wanted the bottle of nail varnish that Becca had worn that day. They didn't spell it out but I assumed it was because they'd found traces of nail varnish on Davies and needed to match it to Becca. That hit home hard – it was something I didn't like to even think about because it brought to mind such horrific images of what might have happened; of them struggling and of him overpowering her. But I couldn't for the life of me think which one it was. Everything appeared to be moving so fast and I seemed to be thinking, thinking, thinking – so much so that I could barely gather my thoughts at all.

'Can you remember which one it was?' I asked Jessica distractedly.

She immediately spread her fingers out in front of me. Her nails were painted pink, though by now they were badly chipped. 'It's this colour,' she said. 'Definitely. Because she painted mine first,' which had us all in tears again, as Jess explained that, because Becca had painted them for her, she wanted them to stay like that forever.

We couldn't seem to find one that was an exact match, however, so in the end, I gave them all the bottles of nail varnish that were on her dressing table, leaving more gaps in the fabric of the room.

I kept telling myself that it was what Becca would have wanted anyway. I could almost hear her saying it – reminding me of her passion to be a barrister – and knowing that meant I could feel her driving me on.

Though it had been John who'd originally asked for it, it was Charmaine who was now assigned the job of thoroughly reading Becca's diaries. I'd already given him her most recent one but with her having kept one for so many years, the 'it' was, in fact, a 'them'. There were diaries that went back to when she was just eight years old; pretty floral little-girl's diaries, which, thankfully, they didn't need. But there were also several big hardback notebooks, from when she'd started in high school, filled with page after page of densely packed writing. Again, I handed the rest of them over sadly, but still willingly. It was important they read them in case there was anything in them that might be relevant to the investigation. Once again, given they were such a personal thing, I was just so grateful that it was Charmaine who'd be doing it.

'Do you think there might be something useful in there?' Charmaine asked me when she came to pick them up.

'I don't know,' I said honestly. 'I've never read any of them.' And, as I went on to tell her, I wouldn't have dreamt of doing so, ever. Though I did often act as safekeeping for them, particularly when she was going out with Davies.

'He was obsessed with seeing them,' I explained to Charmaine, 'obsessed with finding out what she might have written about him so, whenever he was coming over, she would hand them over beforehand so I could hide them away in my bedroom. Then when he'd gone, she'd have them back so she could write a bit more. It used to drive him mad, not knowing what was in there, I remember her telling me.'

Becca's diaries were definitely something of an obsession with him. On one occasion I remembered, I was up in my bedroom and the pair of them were downstairs but they obviously didn't realise I was in the house at all because I suddenly heard them both thundering up the stairs, Davies in front, with Becca chasing behind him, shouting, '*No*, Josh!'

He burst into my bedroom and I remember the shock on his face on seeing me and how he made up some nonsense about Becca pushing him in there – which, of course, she denied because she hadn't.

'I'm sure he was after her diaries,' I told Charmaine. 'I didn't twig at the time but now it's all beginning to make sense. I wouldn't be at all surprised if there's something in there you can use.'

She hugged them to her and promised she'd take very good care of them. And I could tell by her expression that she thought there might be too.

CHAPTER TEN

HOLDING ON

While Charmaine and John were visiting our house and gathering evidence from Becca's bedroom, there was evidence-gathering going on at Davies's house too. We knew that we wouldn't be given any answers so we knew better now than to ask too many questions, but Charmaine would come over often, bringing pictures to show us – one day even of things they'd photographed in Davies's bedroom.

On that day, she also brought actual evidence, which she gently explained she needed me to identify, if possible, though without removing it from its clear plastic bags. It was a selection of different-coloured hair bands and my heart sank. I'd always bought lots of these for her, in lots of different colours, so she could match the colour of her hair band to her clothes.

And I recognised them. They were the ones she'd been

wearing when she'd left the house that morning. I was afraid to look too closely, in case there was blood on them, but they looked pristine and new. So I asked Charmaine if she'd actually been wearing them because I knew she wouldn't have had her hair tied in a ponytail if she was going to be putting her hood up.

And I needed to know, even if I didn't quite know why. But, of course, Charmaine couldn't tell me.

Charmaine then began showing me pictures. She told me that some of the items they'd found in Davies's bedroom had been hidden behind the back of his computer – a knife, an old gold-effect watch on a chain (which I was sure I recognised as being an old one of my sister's – she was always giving Becca bits of jewellery) and some other jewellery, including a silver ring they wanted to ask about.

'But before I show the next picture to you,' Charmaine said, 'I need to warn you that it has blood on it. But it's not Becca's, Sonia,' she added, seeing my traumatised expression. 'It's been tested and it's not hers, OK?'

She wasn't able to tell me whose blood it was though and, as I looked at the picture of the ring, I couldn't stop thinking that it *was* Becca's blood – that they just didn't want to upset me by telling me.

I tried hard not to think about that. 'Yes, it's his,' I confirmed, wondering what its relevance might be. If it wasn't Becca's blood, whose blood was it? 'And Jess will recognise it too,' I said, 'Davies wore it all that time. She might recognise some of the other things as well,' I added, 'because she's actually been in his bedroom.'

We called her in to look at the pictures then and I was about to get a shock.

'Yes, that's definitely his,' she confirmed, looking at the picture of the ring Charmaine was showing her. 'And I recognise that as well,' she added, when Charmaine showed her the photo of the knife. 'I've definitely seen that knife in his bedroom,' she said. 'And he has another one too. Only it's bigger than that one. The bigger one is the one he threatened me with when I was round there one time with Becca.'

'*What?*' I asked, stunned.

'When was this?' Charmaine asked her.

'It was last year,' Jessica told her. They had all been down his house – Becca, Jessica and Jack – and it had been Becca who'd told him to stop it.

'Do you remember what it looked like?' Charmaine continued.

Jess nodded. 'It was bigger than that one, like I say, and it had a serrated edge. And the handle was different – it was sort of made to look like a rabbit's paw.'

'Do you think you could draw it for us?' Charmaine wanted to know. 'This might be important, so we'd probably also want you to come down to the interview suite at Coity again and make a statement about it too. Is that OK?'

Jessica said it was and I just sat there listening, shocked. We might not know the significance behind everything we were being asked but the picture that was emerging, even if it was mostly based on putting two and two together, was becoming more chilling by the day.

After Charmaine had gone, I told Jessica that, if she remembered anything else – however small or seemingly insignificant – she was to tell me straight away, or to write it down, as it might be important. So many questions, but no answers… Not yet.

October became November, which meant Bonfire Night – a night when Linda and I would normally take the children into Cardiff to watch the big firework display in Cooper's Field. There would be hot dogs and hot chocolate and we'd all have such a great time, but when Roger suggested we do something – if only to give Jessica and Jack some sort of distraction – I said absolutely not. I couldn't bear it.

But he suggested I should think again. 'Think about Becca,' he said. 'She would have wanted you to, wouldn't she?'

And I knew he was right. Becca, had loved her little cousins (as did Jessica and Jack) though they weren't actually cousins, but second cousins. Kayleigh (who looked so like Becca) and her little brothers Daniel and Ciaran, were actually the children of Roger and Janet's son Simon, my nephew, and his wife Paula.

So, thinking of what Becca would have wanted, I had the whole lot of them over in the garden – Linda and Robert, too - and, though it was so hard, I was glad I had relented. We made hot dogs and baked potatoes and let off all the fireworks and though it was painful, at least it made me feel we were doing something for Becca, still lying under that snow-white sheet in the hospital morgue.

Almost every minute of every day I thought of her lying there and though I knew there would be a delay because of the need for a post-mortem, I was so anxious to see her moved to the Chapel of Rest. I pestered constantly about when it would be organised and over, so that I could start making the funeral arrangements. But, as if the Davies family hadn't put us all through enough in creating the monster who had killed my daughter, on 8 November, on one of his still-daily visits, John broke the news that their defence team had requested a second post-mortem be done first.

'*What*?' I said, horrified. 'Why?'

'Because they have asked for it,' he said and I realised that was all he could tell me.

'But how can they do that?' I wanted to know. 'What right have they got? The first one was done by a Home Office pathologist – surely his findings should be sufficient? What grounds could they possibly have for cutting up my daughter again?'

'That's just what happens sometimes,' he explained. 'Sometimes they just want to see if they can find anything new.'

I burst into tears then, I was so devastated. It just felt like the cruellest thing imaginable and I became hysterical. It was as if killing Becca once hadn't been sufficient, as if they wanted to kill her – to defile her – all over again.

By now I was falling apart, overtaken by a hatred I never knew I was capable of, my feelings towards Davies like wild beasts straining inside me. I would find myself praying for his own horrific death, that he'd suffer as we were suffering and that his family would suffer too, that they would have to go through what we were, every waking moment, for ever more.

How could it be right that the Defence team could do this to us? It felt wrong in every sense. I even wrote to David Cameron asking him personally how it could be allowed but all I received back was a standard-form letter with a Downing Street stamp: nothing from him personally, and nothing with a shred of empathy.

And there was nothing else we could do. Just try hard not to think about what was being done to Becca's body and, instead, concentrate on the fact that in the not- too-distant future Davies would be in court and I could look at him – and his parents, who'd created him, and still hadn't offered a single word of condolence – and, if there was a God, watch him be convicted of my angel's murder.

Within the first few days of Becca's death, John Doherty had asked me if I wanted to go and see the place where she'd been killed. He hadn't put it quite like that, however – he'd asked if we wanted to visit 'the area'. Because how did you phrase such incredibly delicate matters to a devastated family, after all?

At the time I'd said no because I couldn't bear to see or be seen by anyone and all the while the police were conducting their searches and investigations, I knew the press would have been there almost constantly and, if we'd gone there, they would probably have trained their cameras on us as well.

'I think I'll have to,' I'd told him because I knew I would regret it if I didn't, 'but not quite yet, not until everyone else has gone. It needs to be private – I don't want to go till then.'

The thought of going there at all had been hanging over me ever since. It was enough of an ongoing battle to try to block out the images of Becca's last hours and I knew that actually going there – seeing the scene of her murder with my own eyes – would only make the images sharper still. Nevertheless, I felt it was important to visit the place where my daughter spent the last hours of her life so, when John told me the press had gone and the site had been cleared, I agreed that I would finally make the trip.

It was on Wednesday, 10 November that John came and picked us up. I had intended to go on my own but, when I'd told the children where I'd be going, they were adamant that they wanted to come with me and lay some flowers.

I was very unsure. Already they were going through so much – was it really the right thing for them to have to add the scene of their sister's murder to the list of images that they would have to carry around with them for all time? I was in turmoil too because I didn't know what to expect. Would the tent still be there? Might we spot blood or other evidence? I felt sick at the thought. Would any of us cope?

I rang John in a panic and asked him what he thought.

'I'm not in a position to advise you what to do,' he said reasonably, 'but I can reassure you about the site itself. It's been cleared, there's nothing to see that would let you know what's taken place there.'

Still I dithered. But Jack and Jessica were adamant, and perhaps rightly so. 'What about when we're older?' Jess argued, 'and we didn't go and lay flowers for Bec? We might regret it terribly then, mightn't we?'

They had a point and I realised I must put my misgivings aside, although the night before John was due, I was plagued with terrible thoughts and images about what might have happened that day in those dark woods. Was she scared? Did he torment her first by telling her what he was going to do to her? He was so big and strong, and she was so small and weak. She wasn't even athletic – sport had never been Becca's thing – so she would have had no chance of outrunning him in a million years. I had seen for myself the speed at which he could move and knew she wouldn't have stood a chance of escaping.

My guilt was unbearable. Did she cry out for me? Scream for help, terrified, while he attacked her? I had one job on this earth – to care for and protect my children. And I had failed her.

John phoned on the morning of the 10th, offering to come and collect us, but conscious of how hard he worked and how much he had to do, I arranged to phone him when we got there and had Roger and Janet take us to Aberkenfig instead.

It was shocking, getting out of the car, to see just how close we were to Ninnis's house and more shocking still to see just how many flowers had been laid on the pavement by the entrance to the woods. I read a few of the cards and notes, some of which had been fixed to various teddies, and there was also a man's orange checked hoodie with a grey hood laid out on the ground: it looked almost brand new.

I stared at it, stunned and moved to see how much my baby was loved by so many people. 'I wonder who put the hoodie there,' I said to Jess. 'It seems such a shame, it's going to get ruined.'

Jess didn't know but promised she'd try to find out and, once we'd read as many messages as we felt able to, I telephoned John to let him know that we'd arrived.

It was like going to the dentist as a child, or taking a big important test; my nerves were jangling and I felt sick with apprehension.

We were accompanied that day by Becca's head teacher, Mr Manghan, who'd been brought to the scene by John Docherty: when I'd told him of our plans, he had asked me if he could join us to offer prayers, and it was such a lovely gesture – one that I knew Becca would have approved of – that I told him he was welcome to come too. I was glad to have his presence because I knew it would help calm me enough to keep me strong for Jess and Jack despite the churning in my stomach and the thumping in my chest.

The fear I had felt as we got out of the car was visceral. Was it the same fear that Becca had felt when Davies had brought her there? As John and Mr Manghan approached I took Jack and Jess's hands and gripped them tightly, not wanting to let them go, and asked them once again if they were sure they wanted to do this.

We were just starting into the woods when a lady came up to us and explained that she owned the nearby farm. 'I just wanted to let you know that, if you want to come up here again,' she said, 'you're welcome to park here, well away from prying eyes.'

It was such a kind gesture that it helped to calm me down a little more, even though, as I thanked her, I knew beyond doubt that I would never be coming back here again. I just wanted to get it over with and was happy to set off and let John lead the way to the wood's entrance at the side of the lane.

As we walked, I tried to imagine Becca being there. There was a small bank and a big step-up to get into the woods and I knew she would never have attempted it on her own – and not willingly. 'There's no way Becca would have climbed this,' I told John, as he held out his hand to help me up. 'Not with those boots she'd been wearing!'

It was a feeling that persisted as we went down again – about 4ft, and steeply – before finding ourselves once again on level ground. *There was just no way*, I kept thinking. *She must have been forced. Did he have a knife? Did he have help?*

I was lost in thought when John stopped at a clearing and looked at me. 'Is this it?' I asked him. 'Is this where you found her?'

He nodded and pointed to a tree. It was just a tree among

many trees and I stared at it for a few moments, before nudging the children towards Roger and Janet and then heading off to the far side of the clearing.

'Be careful!' John called. 'There are deep quarries over there!' But I ignored him and walked to the very edge of the gorge, feeling my stomach lurch at the thought of Davies throwing Becca into it, then striding off again to see the rest of the area. It was like a compulsion; I had to see everything with my own eyes, get my own sense of what might have happened that day, not just hear about it from others. See if there was anything, anything at all, that I could spot.

When I returned, Jack was also searching the site, calling to John, telling him about Coke cans and beer cans and crisp packets; asking him to take them for forensic testing. I took his hand, so upset for him, and gently explained to him that they had already taken everything they needed. I then grilled John a little, wanting to know as much as he could tell us. Like where they'd found the weapon, where Becca had been lying, which way she'd been facing, and wondering about how clean and undisturbed everything looked, with its fine golden coat of fallen pine needles.

'It didn't look like this then,' he explained. 'The ground here was very overgrown with brambles and there were rocks and all kinds of things around.'

So it was true: they really had cleared it. Wiped it clean of all the evidence of the horror that it had witnessed, right down to sawing and taking away branches. I laid my flowers then, called the children to me and arranged them where Becca's heart would have been, then blew a kiss to where her face was and bowed my head. And as Mr Manghan started to say prayers and bless the area with holy water, I felt all my anger, confusion and sadness lift away.

I don't know if the clouds had parted at that moment specially but I also became aware that the sun was shining down on us, sending its rays through the gaps in the tops of the trees and illuminating the ground where Becca had lain. It also shone on the hundreds of fine golden needles that were gently floating down on us, like a shower of golden snow. We all stood in silence, bewildered but so thankful to have been given this; it felt like a sign from above, sent to offer us some peace.

It didn't last long but I knew that I would never forget it because the visions I'd carried – of Becca lying in a cold dark forest – had now been replaced by that of a peaceful golden paradise, one that had now been blessed by holy water and where no evil could happen again.

I wanted to leave then and leave quickly while it still looked so lovely, knowing my last image would be of a place that had been cleansed.

I would never return there again.

Becca's body was formally released on 11 November 2010 and we could at last start making arrangements for her funeral. It was actually a relief to have something other than Davies to focus on, to have something in my head every day when I woke up other than the despicable thing he had done to her.

Now it was going to be about her, I was determined. About Linda and me and the children making everything right for her, doing things exactly the way she would have wanted them. But at the same time I was terrified about the day itself and how I was going to get through it. I was so conscious of my responsibility to Jessica and Jack now. Not to mention Linda, who loved her every bit as much as we did. I had to be strong for them, I mustn't crack; I had to hold it together.

I was also fearful of who might turn up. There were no rules about who could or couldn't attend a funeral and I was getting worried about who might decide to come. Though the press had mostly been kind to us, respecting our privacy and the police's request that they should give us space and not hound us, it had been in the news and everyone locally knew all about it.

Friends and neighbours, old and new, had been fantastic. People had brought pies and casseroles to ensure we ate and the children's friends were round constantly, which, with Jessica and Jack in such distress, was incredibly helpful. Becca's friends, too, were such a support, providing distraction when it was needed but also other people to talk to, people who wanted to talk about Becca, which was all any of us wanted to do, to keep her close to us.

The staff at Jack's school were brilliant: his teachers called round often – most of them had taught all three of my children – and Miss Browne and Miss Allen, in particular, were wonderful. Popping in, or phoning, just to see if there was anything they could do.

But there was a wider world out there and this had been a horrible, vicious murder and I knew that, although some would want to be there to support us, others might have more prurient interests, and I feared that, with the investigation still ongoing into her killer, there might be a scene, or worse, a brawl. Quite apart from anything else, with Davies maintaining that Ninnis had killed Becca, I imagined there would be huge antagonism between all the families involved.

I was really anxious about that because the only thing I

wanted was a celebration of my angel's short life on this earth – not a spectacle for those who'd read all about it in the newspaper to gawp at.

And it seemed I was right to be concerned. Almost immediately after the date had been provisionally arranged, Charmaine called round with shocking news.

'I've got to ask you,' she said, 'on behalf of the Davies and Ninnis families, if they'll be allowed to come along and pay their respects.'

I was stunned. 'Why would they think that would be OK?' I said, gaping at her. 'They have not sent a word of condolence – not one. And it was the Davies's son who was responsible for killing Becca!'

'I suppose they think it's the right thing to do,' she suggested. 'And I think the Thomas family want to come as well.'

'How *dare* they?' I said. 'How dare they even suggest that! It's going to be bad enough having to have the Aylward family attending but to think the family of the boy who killed her might be there – the family who are trying to get him off as we speak! They can't be there, I just can't bear it. And I don't want to see the others there either.'

'Don't worry,' Linda said, 'I bet they won't want to be there in a million years – they're probably just saying that because they think it's the right thing to do.'

'And you don't need to worry anyway,' Charmaine added, giving me the answer I needed to hear. 'I'll tell them they won't be welcome and mustn't come. I'm sorry – I had to ask, but I absolutely agree with you.'

Desperate as I had been to get Becca back and start planning her funeral, when it came to it, I found myself in bits again. The local funeral directors, Owen E. Jones, were an old family firm in Maesteg who did everything personally, always coming to the bereaved family's home to arrange everything. Already I'd had one conversation with our funeral director, Gareth, and liked him, but when his car pulled up outside on an afternoon in early November, I had a sort of fugue and couldn't bring myself to let him in.

Jack and Jess had gone to play with their cousins but Linda was with me, thankfully, or I might not have gone through with it. I might just have hidden till he went away again.

'I can't do this,' I told Linda as I watched him get out of his car. He was very smartly dressed and carrying a big briefcase, making it all so horribly real.

'Yes, you can,' Linda quietly insisted. 'I'm here. You'll be OK – we'll do it together and I can be your voice.'

She squeezed my hand and went to the door to let Gareth in. And he was so nice: so gentle, patient and compassionate, handing me books of caskets, books of flowers, ideas for Order of Service booklets, explaining each option with his quiet, measured voice. But just looking at them made my eyes swim – how could I even begin to make choices when I couldn't accept the fact that my little girl was never coming home again?

'Do I have to choose now?' I asked him and he told me that, no, I could have a think first. 'But if you wanted a special casket, or something a bit different, they are all handcrafted, obviously, so would take a little longer to make.'

It felt so unreal, discussing caskets, and I couldn't believe I was doing it – discussing the design of a box in which to bury my 15-year-old daughter, my first-born child.

But it had to be done and, with Linda's help, I made the choices I needed to make. A pure white coffin, the choice of flowers and the Order of Service, which, as Becca had been a devout Catholic, would be a church service with a full requiem mass, to be held at the church attached to her old primary school, Our Lady and St Patrick's RC Church.

It seemed fitting that we'd have the service there, so in that, at least, there was no decision to make. After all, it had been her favourite school and where she'd been at her happiest and most carefree during her childhood. She loved all the teachers and they loved her too.

'I'll make all the arrangements with Father Meredith,' Gareth assured me, then he went on to say that as this was a child and such a tragedy, he wouldn't be charging me for his own services. I would only have to pay for the things we ordered.

I couldn't believe Gareth's kindness, or that of his mother and wife, who looked after Becca in the Chapel of Rest and dressed her in the clothes we had chosen. Jess and Linda also made a trip to Llandaff Cathedral, to buy her a crucifix from the little shop there, which Becca had always loved visiting, plus a little guardian-angel charm to hold in her right hand. For the other, as she'd always loved bangles so much, we chose a 'Jesus band', with little squares on it containing images from the Bible. All these, along with a letter from us all and some precious photos, would travel with her to the better place I knew she'd be going, to be reunited with her gran and granddad.

I chose the flowers for the funeral with her writings in mind, mindful of the plans she'd made all that time back for her wedding. I ordered her name, 'Becca', to be made up of tiny white carnations, dark red roses and baby's breath (gypsophila). The white flowers were there to represent her purity and innocence, and the roses and baby's breath because she loved them.

For the casket, Linda bought her the pure-white lilies and glossy foliage that she had said she'd have liked for her bridal bouquet. From Jessica, we chose the Gates of Heaven, also made with delicate white flowers, and from Jack, a beautiful white floral bear, to represent Angel, Becca's favourite teddy.

Finally, after much thought, I ordered a pure white handcrafted coffin to represent Becca's innocence. Specially made, it would have a gold crucifix at the top and would be draped with gold rosary beads. Becca had lots of rosary beads at home, so I knew this was something she would have wanted.

The last thing to be done was to set the date: 18 November 2010. It was the day I would have to bury my own child; something I never, ever thought I'd be doing in my lifetime and something no parent should ever have to do.

I was dreading it. Much as it mattered that every detail was perfect, this would also be the second-worst day of my life. After three weeks in hell, it would be the day I dreaded the most: the one in which I'd have to let my daughter go.

CHAPTER ELEVEN

GOODBYE, MY DARLING

The week before Becca's funeral passed in a kind of blur – an incredibly busy blur, in which so many family members were involved, pulling together, supporting us and being such a huge source of strength. But there was one aspect of the funeral that hung over everything, even though everyone was loath to bring it up. And that was Becca's father, John Aylward.

Becca would have been 16 on 28 February 2011 and her intention to change her name legally was really just a formality. She was already known as Oatley – my maiden name – at school. It was how she signed her name and what she wrote in her school books, as did both Jessica and Jack. Rebecca hated the name Aylward – her 'biological father's name', as she put it.

At lunchtime on the day before the funeral, the family had begun to gather in my home, the plan being to travel together to the Chapel of Rest at four, to pay our last respects privately.

It was shortly after they'd arrived that I heard what sounded like the letterbox. I went into the hall, thinking it was another family member, or perhaps a sympathy card, but when I picked it up and opened it, it was typed and official looking. And it had obviously been hand delivered, which seemed strange.

As I went back into the living room I started opening it and pulled out a letter that looked equally official. I opened it and began to scan it in the living-room doorway, becoming more incredulous with every line I read.

'It's from the court,' I told everyone, 'and addressed to me and the funeral directors, so I presume a copy's gone to them as well.' I continued to read, not quite believing the words in front of me. It was explaining that there was a hearing set to take place in a court in Cardiff, at 3.30pm that same day, to determine whether the funeral could even go ahead.

'But that's only a couple of hours away!' said Linda, alarmed. 'Can they do that?'

It seemed they could. Or rather, my ex-husband could. At least, he could try and it seemed he had decided to. I continued to read the contents of the letter: he had a long list of demands he wanted met, including time for him and his family alone with Becca before 'permission' to hold the funeral – a funeral he had not offered a penny towards the cost of – would be granted by the courts.

His first demand was that Becca's place of rest was to be changed. It was not permitted for her to be buried with my parents, as we had planned, but somewhere else – laid to rest on her own. It was also stipulated that he would 'allow' me to put some words on her headstone, which angered and distressed me greatly – who was he to 'allow' me to do anything? This was my child he was talking about, my own flesh and blood.

He was also adamant that her headstone read Rebecca Sarah Aylward, something that was only going to happen over my dead body. To allow that would be the ultimate betrayal of my daughter. I would have her headstone engraved with *Rebecca Sarah Oatley*, just as everything else was, and no law in the land was going to stop me.

Nobody spoke for the moment after I finished reading. I think everyone was just so shocked that he could do something like that on such a day. We were all due to visit Becca at the Chapel of Rest that afternoon so to do such a thing seemed inexplicable. It felt like some sick black comedy, the whole idea of us all having to race to the law courts in such a ridiculous undignified style, not to mention the fact that there were two other children – *his* children – involved in all this. I needed to be at home, looking after them, not dashing off to do battle with him. But I was determined he would not get his way. There was no way I was going to allow this to happen so, while Linda used the mobile to phone Charmaine and fill her in, I got straight on the phone to my divorce solicitor, Philippa, the solicitor who had handled my divorce.

Charmaine answered quickly and, once Linda explained what had happened, said she and a colleague were going to head straight to Cardiff Central Station, to try and ward my ex-husband off. In the meantime, Philippa said she would get on to it immediately and that I should come down to her office without delay.

While we rushed down to town, Philippa went straight to work, first phoning the court to explain that it was impossible for me to get to Cardiff in so short a time and that the funeral had already been arranged. Then, while my brother Roger drove me to her office in Maesteg, she faxed information to the judge from our previous contact hearings and arranged a conference call to take place directly with the court proceedings once they commenced.

By the time we arrived at Philippa's office it was close to 3pm and what followed was a very intense hour. Philippa first tried to get hold of the judge but, as he wasn't available, she liaised with another court official and, after endless phone calls and faxes, managed to sort everything out.

It felt surreal to have to do this less than 24 hours before Becca's funeral and it was terribly sad to be in the middle of such a horrible situation. But this was my daughter's funeral I was arranging and despite his attempts to stop me, I was not going to let my ex-husband win. And by late afternoon the court settled in our favour: the funeral *would* go ahead as planned and the only concession was that he would be allowed 10 minutes with Becca at the Chapel of Rest that evening.

I felt so relieved but, after speaking to Gareth at the funeral directors, I also felt anxious, because he had received the same letter. He reassured me, however. He said that, though in all his years he'd never come across anything like it, he would be sure to maintain complete control.

All of which *was* very reassuring but it wasn't long before I realised that this was a situation that would take a great deal of controlling. We were the first to arrive, Linda, the children and me, together with Roger and Janet, and Gareth took us straight to the chapel. Already there were flowers laid out, ready for the funeral, and the chapel itself couldn't have been more calm and peaceful. I'd asked for Becca's coffin to be closed because, though it distressed me not to actually see her for one last time, Gareth had strongly advised against doing so and I trusted his judgement.

Becca was resting to the right of the chapel under a crucifix and we all gathered around her, silent and alone with our thoughts. But after only a short time, Gareth came in, pulled me aside and quietly explained that my ex-husband and his sisters had now arrived too.

'I'm going to take them into another room and talk to them about respect and behaviour,' he said, 'and then I'll be back to you.'

I said OK, and returned to the casket and the children and we had a few more precious minutes of peace. But when Gareth returned for a second time, he took me to one side and said, 'Your ex-husband has asked that he and his sisters be allowed to have ten minutes with Becca alone.'

The rest of my family began filing out then but I shook my head. 'I'm sorry,' I said, 'but I'm not leaving her alone with him.'

He was just about to speak when Jack said, 'I'm staying with Mam and Becca,' and then Jessica joined in: 'I am, too.'

Linda stayed as well and we returned to the head of the casket while Gareth went back outside to fetch them. And when they came in, I could read my ex-husband's expression – although I didn't need to.

'What are you looking at?' he snapped, glaring at me.

'Please, not here,' Linda said. 'Not in *here*.'

I think you go a bit mad in such a horrible situation – I was already mad with grief, of course, but now I had to deal with another set of powerful emotions. I had to deal with being in the same room with someone with whom I'd had such a turbulent relationship for so long, but I had to hold myself together. *I must not become hysterical, particularly in the face of my children's distress*, I told myself.

By now my ex-husband and his relatives were all crying and I had to bite my tongue to stop myself saying anything. I had to concentrate so hard on my children and their needs, just to stop myself from yelling at them to leave her alone.

My ex-husband turned to Jack, then. 'Don't worry, Jack,' he said. 'I know your mind has been poisoned against me but you know I'm still your dad.'

Jack was just nine and I'll never forget his response to this. He was so young still and so upset, yet his voice was so clear and calm. 'You call yourself a father?' he asked him. 'You are no father of mine. You disgust me! How dare you come in here upsetting us all and being disrespectful to MY SISTER!' He looked towards the casket then and pointed, his eyes brimming. 'YOU should be in there, not Becca!' he said. 'Why don't you just *go*?'

It was the first time I had ever seen my ex-husband lost for words. His sisters rallied round him, patting him on the back and telling him that it would all be all right. *All right?* I thought. *I have to bury my child tomorrow. How can anything 'be all right' ever again?*

One of his sisters closed the curtains around the casket to block our view then. Incensed, I pulled them back again. 'They stay open,' I said and thankfully nobody argued with me. By now, having heard Jack, who had started sobbing, the rest of my family returned to the chapel, Linda going straight to him and drawing him into her arms, while I silently prayed that the situation wouldn't get any worse.

But it did. On seeing Linda, my ex-husband shouted, '*You!*
You're the one that drove her to her death!'

Sickened, I immediately jumped to my sister's defence,
asking how he could even think of saying such a wicked thing,
which I hoped would bring the focus of his anger back to me,
where it belonged. Not on Linda, and not with my poor
distressed children present and my Becca right beside us, laid
supposedly to rest.

I had had enough, I decided. There was to be no more of this.
I had the mobile phone the police had given me in my bag, so
I got it out and passed it to Linda. 'That's it,' I said. 'Can you
please go out and call the police for me and ask them to have
him taken away? He is not upsetting my children any more.'

By this time, Gareth was already trying to remove my ex-
husband anyway. And he was still trying to do so when, in what
seemed no time at all, the police themselves arrived. They'd had
a riot van parked around the corner, ready.

'My brother-in-law's not been in yet,' my ex-husband
protested as they took him away. 'I want my brother-in-law to
be allowed to go in!'

But it was not allowed, and we had a few more precious
moments with Becca before her body was removed to the
church by the school, ready for the funeral, and we held a Mass
for her. And there we had to leave her. And, though I knew she
was safe in God's House, it was such a wretched thing to have
to do.

There is probably nothing in the world that can compare to
the visceral pain of having to attend your own child's funeral.
Together, as a family, we had planned every last detail with one
aim – to make sure Becca's send-off wasn't dark or sad and

morbid but rather a celebration of her life. We had the whole church lit up brightly and the hymns were all celebratory – the ones that Becca had always loved singing when attending Mass herself. It was hard to believe that it had only been 10 years before that she'd been in this very church being baptised.

We tried our best to keep the tone as uplifting as we could too, going afterwards to the local Catholic Hall – a place where we'd spent many happy family times and where we'd placed a memory book full of photos and keepsakes. It was good to have the focus – something to occupy our ravaged minds – but the day itself, now that the work was done and all the details were in place – was, and still remains, a blur of agony.

She was gone, this was it: *she was gone*. And now we had to find a way to live the rest of our lives without her.

PART TWO

CHAPTER TWELVE

KINDNESS AND COURTROOMS

.

After the funeral was over I knew I had to get myself to a new place emotionally. Currently, everything was jumbled up together. I was trying to grieve for Becca side by side with raging against her murderer – waking up each day with such a horrible jumble of violent images and feelings of fury and despair.

So I took action. When we'd visited the crime scene, I'd been deeply touched by all the flowers and messages and tokens that had been left there. Lots of teddies, in particular, and because Becca had always loved teddies, I wanted them at her place of rest, not at the scene of her murder – that was the last place I wanted any sort of shrine to her. I had already had them gathered up and now I took them to the cemetery so they could sit on her grave.

There was also the orange and grey hoodie that had been left at the entrance to the woods. Jess had managed to find out that it had belonged to a lad called Gabriel, a friend of Becca's, and when I got in touch with him, he explained why he laid it there.

'She always loved it on me,' he told me, 'always commented on how nice it looked. So it just seemed the right thing to do – to leave it for her.'

I was so moved, I could hardly speak but when I did, it was to let him know that I'd taken it away and brought it home and I hoped he wouldn't mind. 'Because it's the place Davies chose to kill her,' I explained, 'and we want to take that power away from him – remove all traces of Becca being there. So if you are happy for me to, I'd like to wash it and press it [it had been rained on by now, of course] and put it in her wardrobe with the rest of her clothes. She's everywhere at home,' I added, 'and you and your friends are always welcome to come round and feel close to her.'

Gabriel didn't mind, so that was exactly what I did, and I felt all the better for it.

I needed to feel better – at least, as well as I possibly could – because I knew my main job was to support Jack and Jessica through the coming weeks and months. I still felt numb with shock but at the same time my mind was just too full of everything; the ordeal of having to bury my baby, the stress of the legal dispute with my ex-husband and just the sheer magnitude of what we all had to face every morning: trying to come to terms with something I felt we'd never be able to accept as long as we lived.

I was still in the dark about almost everything to do with the ongoing investigation. Though the police were in touch constantly, asking for further information, they still told me almost nothing in return. I would ask questions and their reply was always the same: that they would go and find out the answer and get back to me, if and when they could. Which of course they never did, although I did understand. After all, this was a murder investigation and I was a principal witness. One slip-up in sticking to the rules about what I could and couldn't be told, and Davies could walk away on a technicality.

That there was still a lot for me to find out was becoming increasingly evident by the day – that was obvious just from the sheer volume of questions that they were asking. This, I was now clear about, was no crime of passion, no spur-of-the-moment act of random violence, and once we got to court, I would find out everything I was burning to know. *More* than I would want to know probably and my FLOs tried to prepare me for that ordeal as well. I would have to sit in court and listen to things that I really didn't want to hear and I knew I'd have to try and get myself strong enough to be able to deal with it. Because if there was one thing that was going to happen when Davies went to trial, it was going to be that I would be there too, listening to every word – particularly when he was on the stand giving his evidence. Already I knew enough to be sure it was all going to be lies but I also knew *him*, and better than many did. His body language would tell me all I needed to know.

Helping the police was at least something to distract me from the coming ordeal and I put my energy into getting them any useful information I could. And by now there was lots of information coming my way because everyone at Becca's school talked about the case endlessly. Her close friends, who still came round to visit us regularly, would often tell me things they'd heard, both before and after Becca's murder, and though many of these were accounts of things they'd had reported to them rather than heard themselves, one consistent picture was emerging: that Joshua Davies had talked about killing Becca to several people over a period of many months before he did so.

One of Becca's 'close' friends, Megan James, also unwittingly led me to some information that might potentially be useful as well. She'd been in touch with me on Facebook regularly, since finding out about Becca's death, sending me poems, words of comfort, promises that her best friend would never be forgotten, but then one day she admitted that Davies had written to her and that, despite being 'a hundred per cent behind Becca', she told me she had written back to him.

I knew Davies was not allowed to write to anyone, and said so, but the girl admitted he'd sent it to her via his mother and that one of his younger brothers had passed it on. Suddenly, the mutual support between us had vanished. I told the police, who immediately seized the letter.

Things like that made it so clear just how careful we had to be in order not to jeopardise a conviction based on a legal technicality. And clearer still that Joshua Davies still managed to cast some sort of spell over the young people around him, even from his remand cell.

Though it would be a long time before the relevance of this 'hold' over people would become a chilling piece in the much larger jigsaw, at the end of November I found some more evidence of it myself. I'd been up late at night – it was so hard to sleep still – and was looking through old MSN conversations between Davies and Becca.

Above left: The Gates of Heaven memorial stone where Rebecca is laid to rest with my Mam and Dad, who will look after her until we are reunited.

Above right: Rebecca having a break from revising for her Science exam to take one of the many selfies she used to take of herself.

Below: This shows the route that Davies made Becca walk in order to have her seen in the area near where Josh Humphreys lived. She eventually went past the street where Davies lived and up to Church Street, where she met that monster.

Above: One of our many family days out to Stratford-upon-Avon. We saw David Tennant – Becca's favourite actor – play Hamlet and she loved it so much that we saw it again the following week.

Below left: Becca and Jess are pictured here in one of the hundreds of selfies Becca took on her phone. I recently found that she had saved many to disc, which I am so thankful for.

Below right: A sketch Becca did of herself in 2009. As well as reading she loved to draw – mainly people, but her favourite was to make designs for new clothes.

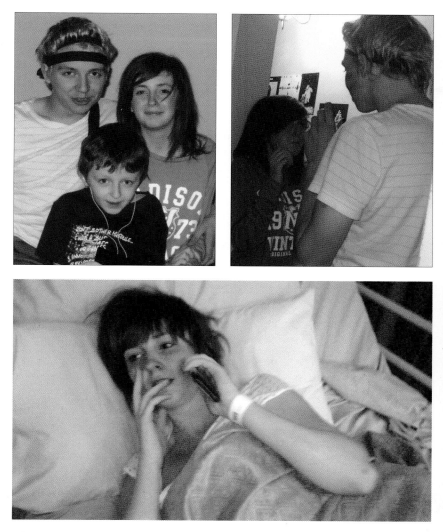

Above left: This photo, one of many of Davies at our house, was taken during a long weekend Davies spent with us. Right after this photo I remember him saying this was the best time he'd had in his life, but an hour or so after he got back to his house he ended the relationship.

Above right: This photo speaks volumes. You can see how petite Becca is compared to Davies; he towers over her.

Below: The doctors admitted Becca to hospital after an unexplained illness caused numerous blackouts in 2010. She really was unwell but not once did Davies visit her at hospital or phone any of us asking how Becca was.

Right: I love this photo of my girls, they were singing and dancing to Christmas songs and everything was just perfect.

Left: We all loved rugby, especially when Wales played and it has always been a major event in our home, with a buffet, drinks and sore throats afterwards. Becca was so proud when Jack scored a try in his first ever game for Maesteg Welsh.

Right: All of my children loved the snow and spent many hours out building snowmen and having snowball fights in the garden. What they would really look forward to though was the hot chocolate I would have waiting for them when they came in.

Frustratingly, in this case, I only had half the conversation because – as was often the case with teenagers at that time – they were communicating by MSN and text message concurrently. And it soon became clear that Becca was responding on MSN to messages he was sending her by text.

I scrolled down the screen, increasingly horrified, reading things like 'Jess and me will never be on our own'. It seemed from these exchanges that he was threatening to hurt both Becca and Jessica at a party I'd arranged for them and their friends at the Zone nightclub in Maesteg (which also ran teenage parties) on 2 October. Because of what I'd already heard from several of Becca and Jess's friends, I realised this could be a key bit of evidence. So, although it was 11.30pm, I knew the police would want to hear about it. I phoned Charmaine and, as ever, she was on duty in the Incident Room, keen to hear what it was I'd turned up.

'OK,' she said when I explained what I'd found. 'Someone will be in touch with you in the morning. And in the meantime, don't do anything to the computer, will you? Don't accidentally delete anything you've found.'

I groaned. 'You're going to want to take my laptop now, aren't you?'

'I'm sorry,' she said. 'But I'm afraid so, yes.'

I was gutted because this meant I wouldn't be able to collect any more evidence. Already they had Becca's and Jessica's computers; now they would have mine as well. I spent the next couple of hours hunting down blank DVDs and saving everything I could think of that might matter.

And there was more of it as well. The picture that was emerging was truly horrifying. It seemed Davies had made all sorts of threats to kill people. I found another conversation he had on MSN with Becca, in which he told her that next time Aylward (Becca's father) came up to the house to invite him in, to 'get that lot' (meaning me, Jess and Jack) out of the house and then he would 'kill him'.

There was also another piece of evidence that obviously mattered – the knife Jessica had already mentioned Davies threatening her with. So, on 2 December, with the case well underway, Jess had to be taken to the Coity interview suite to be interviewed on camera and to make a further statement about it.

Unlike me, she had been in Davies's bedroom. She'd also been able to dig out some photos of the sorts of things in there, including various knives, guns and swords. Looking at the pictures of his bedroom was an enlightening experience. Though Charmaine and John had already told me about a few of the things they'd found in there and taken away as evidence, it was only now that I could see the extent of what seemed to be an obsession with all things dark and dangerous.

Christmas was approaching and it tortured all of us. I hated the sight of fairy lights being strung up, the sound of carols being played in shops, the smiles on everyone's faces as they ran around buying presents. As far as I was concerned, there could be no Christmas in our house – not without Becca, who'd loved it so much. And she *had* loved it; Christmas had always been so special for her. She'd always made it her job to set the table so beautifully and, way before that, she'd be the one to get down all the decorations and who'd supervise Jess and Jack as they decorated the tree, all giggling and singing Christmas songs together.

Becca was our little Christmas planner and without her, we were all at sea. Just thinking of the little notes she used to write – little to-do lists of things we needed to buy or needed to organise – was enough to make us want to climb into bed and weep and not come out till the whole thing was over.

Once again, I had to shut myself off from even thinking about it. I focused, instead, on what was due to happen on 8 December; that was when Joshua Davies was due to appear again in court. He was to attend Bridgend Magistrates Court for a second time, to be committed to Crown Court, and this time I fully intended to be there.

I had no idea where Davies was being held but that was probably a good thing. By then I harboured such hatred for him that I might not have been able to trust myself not to do something stupid. I was also outraged by his family, of whom I'd seen or heard practically nothing since the day their son killed my daughter: one thing I had found out was that they were still protesting his innocence.

Going to court is a singular experience. For the first time, Linda, Roger, Janet and I were in extremely close proximity to 'the enemy'. That's how it felt, at any rate, because not only were we in the same building as the person I knew had murdered my daughter but also his family and supporters. So it was, perhaps, sensible that we were quickly whisked away to a room that was reserved solely for us because, with everything I'd learned, the anger I was feeling by this time was at boiling point.

I managed to keep it together, though, not least in part because of our Victim Support Officer, Ross. He was brilliant; an ex-police officer, he was a mine of information as well as being an incredible support. I also had my wonderful divorce solicitor Philippa on the premises – she was in court with another client and stopped by to show her support, for which kindness I was so grateful.

Once in the court, it was a different matter. It seemed there was no equality when it came to who could and couldn't be present because, while Davies was allowed to have his family with him in court, only one member of Becca's family was permitted. There was a reason for this, obviously, because the law is very clear on how it works: it was the state prosecuting Davies, not me or my family, and as the defendant – innocent until proven guilty, obviously – he had rights in terms of his wellbeing and support. But I would defy anyone in my position – as the mother of the girl who had been so brutally murdered – not to feel a huge sense of injustice in all this. It was as if my child – who I'd just buried – didn't matter much at all.

'This can't be right,' I protested as the usher explained that only one of us – i.e. me – would be allowed in. Already I was on the edge just at the thought of so much as glimpsing Davies – every time someone went in and out of the room we were in, I had to look away in case I saw him being brought into the court. It was a mixture of dread and anger that I knew I'd struggle to control if I was made to go into court and face him alone. 'I'm not going in there on my own,' I explained to Ross, our Victim Support Officer. 'I *can't* go in there on my own – I *have* to have somebody with me.'

Ross went away to make enquiries and to my great relief, was soon back saying that I could take Roger in as well, though not Ross himself – ironically, the 'support' bit obviously stops at the courtroom door.

'But his parents won't be sitting with him,' Ross explained after Roger asked where they'd be. 'He'll be brought in by guards where he's being held on remand and will be sitting with them.' Which was a comfort, albeit a scant one.

Going into that courtroom in Bridgend was a taste of what was to come and I was glad to go in and find it quite small. There were no more than twenty seats, in two rows, with a walkway and steps between them. I couldn't see Davies's parents but I knew they could see me – I was sitting with the major-crimes officers, wearing my white BECCA hoodie: white to represent her innocence, just like her coffin, and with her name and a pink heart on the back. I'd bought it specially and wearing it helped to give me strength – it was a little something I could do for her, knowing that Davies would see it. And I wasn't prepared to let him forget; I wanted her name imprinted on his brain every second of every day. And as soon as I got in the room, I wished I had a picture of her printed on the front as well so that every time he looked up, he'd be forced to see her face.

Joshua Davies entered the court via a side room. He walked up a flight of steps that were no more than four feet from me, and along a short walkway – all of it protected by glass – to the dock where he would stand and face the judge.

A lot of legal talk began then but I struggled to hear any of it because I was so fixated on his face. It was pale and puffy and he looked rough, as if, perhaps, he'd been on the end of one of the beatings he seemed so keen on inflicting on others during the many conversations I'd now read on MSN. 'Scared' – I remembered his words: how he liked people being scared of him. Right then, I couldn't have been less scared or any angrier.

Had I been able to get through those tall panes of glass, I think I might have killed him with my bare hands.

He was dressed in clothes that had presumably been given to him – clothes to make him look smart and vulnerable and benign. But no amount of clothing could disguise the lack of emotion on his face as both the charge and Becca's name were read out.

It's almost impossible to explain how much I wanted to kill Joshua Davies when I saw him enter the courtroom that day; perhaps only someone who has lost a child to a murderer in such circumstances can really understand. I knew there would be no death penalty for him to face; not even a life sentence that would actually *mean* life – and the way I saw it, anything less than that would be too good for him. Why should he serve time in prison to then be allowed to come out and live a normal life? Enjoy freedom, perhaps get married, have a wife and children of his own, while my own child had had her life taken by him? *Why?* I couldn't understand how this could be right or fair at all.

No one wants to feel that way – it's so all-consuming and corrosive. Above everything, it eats into your soul. But knowing what he did to her and that he was still alive while she was dead was just too terrible a wrong for me to be able to feel anything other than a passionate wish for him to be dead too.

But he wasn't going to die because I wasn't able to kill him. All I could do was wait for justice to be done. Wait and, in the meantime, hope he was suffering. Suffering because he couldn't do his hair the way he wanted; because he couldn't look 'cool' and have everyone fawning round him; because, for the first time since I'd known him, he had to be silent and could only speak when he was spoken to. *I bet he hates that*, I thought, watching him, *not being 'top dog' for a change*. It was his own term, that – something he had often been heard to call himself. *Well*, I thought, *not any more*.

But I knew he must have been told where I'd be sitting and encouraged not to look at me because not once did he so much as glance in my direction. It was only when he was leaving the court and had to walk past me that he looked at me – albeit still behind his protective glass – and his expression was the same as it had ever been whenever he'd come to our house: a smile.

It was a moment that brought me up short. I realised then that it wasn't a smile – it probably never had been. It was a smirk. I'd never stopped to think about it before and, now that I did, I realised he'd had a permanent smirk on his face all the while, just the same as when he'd come to our home. It was *me* who was wrong – I'd just been seeing what I wanted to see. I was so busy always looking for the good in people, rather than the bad, that I'd seen a smile where I should have seen that horrible smirk.

He even looked like he was going to speak to me – to say what, I don't know. But when our eyes met, I gave him a look that *should* have killed him and he obviously thought better of saying anything after all. Instead, seeing his parents sitting in a corner to our right, he stopped and smiled and waved to them instead.

Seeing that, I was appalled. Chilled. I couldn't quite believe what I was seeing. He was looking and behaving as if he didn't have a care in the world. It really was as if he wasn't quite human. I looked at his mother then too and I hated her as well, for being the person who had created such evil, even though she clearly couldn't or wouldn't accept that he'd done what he did. She had known Becca – known her *well* – yet not once since we'd arrived in that courtroom did she give any indication that it mattered to her at all that my child – an innocent 15-year-old girl *who she knew so well* – had been brutally murdered. It beggared belief.

CHAPTER THIRTEEN

BEAUTIFUL BECCA

How do you get through something like Christmas when you're in the middle of a nightmare like we were living? I had no idea. How would anyone? But I think Becca must have been looking down on us all because, as Christmas approached, I could hear her voice in my ears constantly, telling me I must do it for Jack and Jessica. 'Do it for them, Mam,' she was urging. 'They love Christmas too.'

So I did. One day I found sufficient strength to take a deep breath and get a few decorations from the under-stairs cupboards where we'd stashed them when we moved in. I also pulled out our old tree – a distressing business because it was a tree that had seen us through good times and bad. It was a 6ft-tall, bushy Highland fir, which looked incredibly real – even down to the pine cones – and needed very little in the way of decoration other than our string of warm white twinkle lights and the children's homemade baubles and favourite tiny teddies. Becca had really loved that tree – every year we'd go out intending to buy a new one only to come back empty-handed. 'Leave it, Mam,' she'd say. 'Let's keep the one we already have – it's nicer.' And now she'd never see it again.

Jack and Jessica tried their best and it was heart-breaking to watch them, seeing their sad little faces as they hung baubles in virtual silence, knowing they were thinking exactly the same as I was – that their big sister should be doing it with them; that they should have all the Christmas songs blaring from the CD player and be singing along with them, while eating half the chocolate decorations between them, before they even made it to the tree. As a form of torture, it surely ranked among the most effective ever devised.

It was a particularly snowy winter and I was glad of it. Being snowed in meant I had an excuse to hide away, avoid everyone else's Christmas preparations and to do what shopping I needed to do online. I felt Becca's presence constantly; she'd always loved Christmas shopping and, as we lived a long way from Cardiff, her idea of Heaven was to travel up and shop there. Everything I did that Christmas I made myself do for her because I could constantly hear her telling me I had to think of Jess and Jack, to do my best for them.

My main concern was obviously to include her so, just before the day itself, the three of us, plus Linda and my eldest brother Robert made a trip to the cemetery where Becca was laid to rest with my Mam and Dad, taking wreaths, a couple of baskets of Christmas flowers and two little light-up decorated trees, to add to the mass of tributes and flowers already there. Once we were done it looked so beautiful, the twinkling lights of the trees casting coloured patterns on all the drifts of snow. We each took a white balloon as well and, after we'd laid everything, we released them, watching them float up over the trees and, hopefully, to the stars.

We went back a few times more, as it felt so important to be near her and, although it was almost unbearable leaving her out in the cold to return to our warm home, it was, at least, another chance to talk to her; we would light Chinese lanterns and release them as well, carrying little messages from us all and pictures Jack had drawn of some of the things the children always used to do together. And through all this we were supported amazingly: friends and family were popping round almost constantly and our daily contact with John and Charmaine never ceased.

'You don't need to call me tomorrow,' I told John, when he telephoned on the evening of Christmas Eve. 'You need to take a day off yourself.'

'I know,' he said, 'but I just wanted you to know I will be thinking of all of you. Have the best Christmas you can, OK? I know how difficult this will be for you all.'

I was so touched. And he was right, of course – it was extremely difficult. The children opened their presents and we tried our best to hold it together but all any of us really wanted to do was curl up and sleep through the whole thing, only waking up when January came around. But we went to Linda's as we'd planned (it would have been too distressing to cook and eat at home that day) and, along with Robert, we all sat down and had 'a meal' together – the words 'Christmas dinner' having gone the way of so many other everyday expressions we didn't want to hear, like 'celebrate'. I couldn't imagine ever celebrating anything again, other than the day I saw Davies sent to jail.

We thought it would be slightly more bearable being at Linda's, in terms of being a distraction of sorts, but as soon as we sat down, all I could see was the place at the table where Becca had sat the previous Christmas and whenever we went round there for a meal. And away from our own home I had to fight an overwhelming sense of panic that I was away from Becca's presence and all her things. I just wanted to sleep and sleep – that's what I remember most, just wanting to be unconscious. It was the only respite I would ever get from the horrendous thoughts in my head. And though there was the small consolation that Davies was locked in a cell, away from his family, it was a scant one. They could still visit him; his mother could still kiss him and hug him; things I would never – because of what *he* had done – be able to do to my daughter again. I resented his mother that – resented it so much.

But eventually it drew to a close – it felt as if I had willed the clock hands myself – and when midnight came around, it was such a huge relief. *Thank God*, I thought, *thank God it's all over!*

New Year's Eve passed in just the same way.

With a sense of grim determination I approached the start of the coming year. I knew I had only two options: either to focus all my energies on bringing Davies to justice or stay in bed, curl up and wait to die. Some days it was so hard but every morning, however appealing the latter option was, I could hear Becca's voice willing me to get up and carry on. 'Come on,' she'd say. 'Stay strong and fight!'

I was still on my quest to gather any information I could and, as I hardly slept at night, would use the time rooting through the stuff that had yet to be unpacked from our move. As so much had been thrown into boxes – and, of course, subsequently forgotten – I would make unexpected finds and would spend the small hours poring over old notebooks of Becca's, bags of school books and other bits and bobs, even pictures I'd found that she'd drawn of herself and Davies. I'd make copious notes, collect anything that seemed remotely useful and would then text John Doherty, often in the middle of the night, fearful that I might forget something vital by morning.

It got me through, after a fashion, and gave me a badly needed focus, while the process of law rumbled on. On 13 January 2011 the next stage took place in Crown Court – the Plea and Case Management Hearing (PCMH). Davies didn't attend this and neither did I. It was just a hearing for the barristers, the first of many steps to be gone through before the murder trial itself.

From day one I had never doubted the police – why would I? I knew they had placed Davies and Ninnis at the scene – neither boy was denying that – and I knew that because, when they came round on that Sunday afternoon, they'd told me they'd had no doubt at all. But now I was beginning to learn more. Though our hardworking FLOs were unable to enlighten me further, they didn't really need to. I knew because by now everything was starting to fall into place.

In parallel with the police investigation, there was, of course, lots of speculation about what had possessed Davies to do what he'd done that day. And it seemed that, to some, it wasn't as shocking an act as many had initially believed. By now I'd heard the same thing from so many more of Becca's friends – that Davies had apparently talked of killing Becca – and Jess as well, it seemed. I was aghast that no one had ever thought to tell me this because it seemed that it hadn't been said lightly either. He might have been a child in the eyes of the law but he was also a 6ft-tall male with a fascination for the dark and violent, and one thing that kept coming up was the *way* he had apparently talked about it; with a strange, nasty look on his face. And it was obviously something that had stayed in people's memories because, when the police asked Becca's friends who *they* thought might have killed her, almost every one of them, without hesitation, said 'Joshua Davies'.

But hearsay wasn't evidence, not of the quality that was needed anyway and so, though I filed it away in my mind, I had to try and detach myself emotionally; put all my own questions aside and try to concentrate on my loved ones. And not just them either because Becca's murder had touched the whole community: it didn't only affect me, Jess and Jack and our family, it also affected all her friends. While we'd been struggling to cope with every new day, so had they. So, although it was hard, I felt I must help support them too – I knew it was what Becca would have wanted.

Becca's friends visited often – just as they had while she was alive – and I would happily let them sit in her bedroom and reminisce. They seemed to gain comfort from being surrounded by her favourite things and I knew it would help them come to terms with having lost her, so I always welcomed them into our home.

But towards the end of January, I had a call from Dr Mangham, Becca's head teacher, who was becoming increasingly concerned. We'd already spoken a couple of times, particularly about Megan James, the close friend of Becca's to whom Davies had written shortly after the murder and whom I was still trying to support as best I could. Despite my concerns about them writing to each other, I did understand her distress, both at losing one of her best friends since she started high school and because, like me, she didn't understand how Davies – who she'd always liked, I remembered Becca having told me so – could do such a terrible thing.

'Can I do anything to help?' I asked Dr Mangham.

'Well, I was wondering if you'd come into school,' he said. 'Megan spends all her time in the chapel and we're worried about her; she's missing Becca terribly and it's affecting her school work.' And it wasn't just Megan the head was worried about either. Several of Becca's other friends seemed to be struggling as well and spending a great deal of time in the school chapel, where there were Books of Condolence, pictures and candles usually lit, so that people could come and pay their respects.

'We wanted to ask if you'd be prepared to talk to them,' he said. 'Spend some time in the chapel yourself, of course, so you can see all the cards and messages but also be there for her friends – we thought perhaps they could come along there and see you and talk to you. We were hoping you could try to persuade them that what Becca would have wanted was for them to get back to their studies; that it was time they began to think about moving on.'

It was, perhaps, not the best choice of words under the circumstances. I would never 'move on' from this and neither would my family. But I did understand what he was trying to achieve and he was probably right. It *was* what I knew Becca would have wanted. She'd always worked so hard at her own studies and I knew she would want me to encourage her friends to do the same.

Agreeing to visit the chapel and actually going in there were two different things, however, and I asked Linda, Jess and Jack if they would come in as well, as I knew I wouldn't be able to cope on my own. And almost as soon as we drove into school on that January morning, I realised it would be even harder than I thought. This was a school I had been to on countless occasions over the years; I'd gone to every sporting event, every parent's evening, every show. And as we walked along the corridors, I could remember how the teachers would always talk to me, telling me how bright my daughter was, how warm and friendly, how hardworking, how, whatever she chose to do in life, she would surely succeed.

I remembered Becca too, taking me to those same meetings with teachers, pulling me along, proud and excited, to show me where she spent her days, saying 'This is my English class and this is my History class…' And now all of it gone, none of it ever the same again.

I held the children's hands tightly as we walked past the main hall and dinner hall and down the small corridor that led to the chapel. And as we drew closer, I could smell flowers mingled with incense – the same beautiful smell that filled the church at Becca's funeral, a smell I'll never forget as long as I live.

They had made it so beautiful. There were candles burning either side of a photograph of Becca and, as I gazed at the open Condolence Books, further photographs and mementoes, it was all I could do not to turn around and run away from it all as fast as I could. It just felt so raw – like an open wound. Particularly difficult to look at was the big noticeboard close by, which was plastered with further photographs, letters and notes from friends; so many that they overlapped and spread over the board's margins, their edges stirring slightly in the breeze.

It was too much, at that early stage, to even think about reading them and we were glad the Head had organised some private time for us in there, as we all broke down and it took some time to compose ourselves. Then, once we felt able, he told the pupils that we were in the school and they could visit, and that, too, was traumatic because Becca's friends were so distressed themselves.

There was a constant stream of pupils for something like two hours. Some I already knew, of course, and a few I knew really well but there were lots of them that I didn't know and I think we were all overwhelmed just by the sheer volume of young people who wanted to come and see us.

Not that everybody who stopped by was welcome. One of the visitors was Tyler Harry, the boy who Davies's grandmother had raised. John Doherty had already spoken to him about keeping away from us and I was astounded that he would even show his face.

How dare he come in here! I thought, glaring at him as he entered the chapel, bold as brass. I had no idea what would prompt him to do such a thing.

'He's not welcome in here,' I told Jessica. 'Who does he think he is?'

But Jess was one step ahead of me. She had already leapt up from her seat to go and challenge him and he hot-footed it out again before she could let fly. But, thankfully, the visit ended on a positive note. We left the school at around noon and went to lunch with a few of Becca's close friends. It was so nice to spend time with them and escape the reality of home for a couple of hours, and I was pleased to think our visit might have helped some of them a little. I was so deeply touched that Becca had touched the lives of so many people with her warmth and kindness and, seeing this in the huge number of beautiful messages (even if I would have to put off reading the bulk of them for a very long time) really brought it home to me that her time on this earth, though tragically short, had been well spent. She would live on in their hearts and memories, and that was a great comfort.

CHAPTER FOURTEEN

PUBLIC PROPERTY

When you lose someone close to you everyone tells you that the first year is always the worst. We'd done the funeral, we had done Christmas, but now the biggest hurdle loomed. On 28 February 2011 it would have been Becca's 16th birthday.

All bereavement is hard – there's no league table of pain in such matters – but I felt so desolate about losing my daughter in such horrific circumstances. Not only was there no chance to say goodbye and tell her how much we loved her, there was also the interminable and deeply traumatic business of having to spend that desperate first year constantly reliving the nightmare. There was no chance to shut out the horror because we were always giving statements; no chance to have quiet time because we were constantly helping with enquiries. And there was no privacy for any of us because we'd become public property – we were in the middle of a big newsworthy murder investigation and Becca was splashed all over the media. No, they weren't knocking on our door, as they were respecting our privacy, but that didn't stop them from writing about the 'story'. Her little cousins, so bewildered about where she had disappeared to, would see her picture on a newsstand and say 'Becca?' The confusion on their faces was so hard to bear.

But still the need to help convict Becca's killer drove me on. I spent the remainder of January just trying to get on top of everything because, with the trial on the horizon, I didn't want to overlook anything that might prove a vital piece of information. It was a big job: having literally just moved in at the time of Becca's murder, there was still a great deal to be gone through because time had stopped, pretty much, from that day.

And I turned up some potentially good finds; particularly one of Becca's old school bags, which, as well as having notes in it that included Davies's name, also contained old mobile phones of both Becca's and Jessica's, a make-up bag and various other items. There was also a bin bag of ripped-up diary entries that Becca, who'd been sorting out her bedroom ready for moving to our new home, had given me only days before the move itself.

'These are not to be seen by anyone ever,' she'd told me, handing over a large paper carrier containing the heap of shredded paper. 'Anyone at *all*,' she repeated and, seeing enough to know they were things she'd written – probably diary entries – I told her I'd transfer them to a bin bag and keep them safe.

Remembering them now, I retrieved the bag and took a brief look at the contents. Seeing the name 'Josh' cropping up among the many slivers of torn paper, I realised they might contain something incriminating. I called Charmaine immediately and she told me she'd be straight over to get everything – the bin bag, the school bag and the contents of the school bag. Once again, I felt reluctant to let them go. I knew I had to – and this happened numerous times over the coming weeks – but it was like my home was being systematically stripped of every physical, personal thing that connected me to Becca.

'My best birthday present,' I kept remembering Becca telling me, 'will be getting my surname changed to Oatley.' But the day would be marked differently, from a legal perspective. There would be no precious name change for Becca that day but there would be a day in court: the day of 28 February was also the date of Davies's next hearing.

This was to be another PCMH meeting, in Bridgend Magistrates Court, where all the logistics of the coming trial were to be finalised. It was then that I found out where Davies was being held: at a secure unit for young people just outside Bristol. Called Vinney Green, it's a place that houses children and teenagers who have committed very serious crimes. It's tucked away on a housing estate on the edge of the city and the judge was apparently unhappy to hear that Davies would continue to be held there for the duration of the trial. He felt it would be inappropriate, both in terms of cost and inconvenience, to have him travel to and from the court every day, when he could just as easily be held in the local secure unit at HMP Parc.

The defence, however, disagreed, saying it was too close to home. From a cell in Parc Prison you could almost see the scene of the crime and they were very concerned for Davies's safety. A lot of the prisoners incarcerated in Parc Prison were from Maesteg and the surrounding area and would want to take revenge on him for taking the life of a local girl. As it was (something I only found out much later), he was very safe, the story in Vinney Green apparently being that he was in there for GBH and he was kept protected and mostly away from others.

There was much debate but, eventually, the judge decided he could stay in Bristol. He was keen for the trial to go ahead without delay – it had been pencilled in for March – and was also conscious that, if Davies *was* moved to Parc Prison, his defence could argue – even if he wasn't assaulted while there – that he was under duress.

Once again, as the day approached, I felt the hatred well up inside me. And once again, I watched him stand there in a smart pink shirt and school trousers and felt incredulous. It was as if he was a machine, not flesh and blood – there wasn't a shred of human emotion apparent. No sense of guilt for what he'd done, not even a sense of sorrow. Had he been innocent – which I knew he wasn't – surely there would be some hint of that? But there was nothing, just that unsettling blank half-smile on his face. *Yet he knows...* I kept thinking. *He* knows *today is her birthday.*

I didn't take my eyes off him. In fact, I sat sideways in my seat so he'd be more aware of my scrutiny and perhaps feel uncomfortable. Yet there was no sign that he even registered my presence. Yes, he was nervous from time to time – I could tell because I knew him well enough to know that, when he was anxious, he cracked his knuckles – and when he fidgeted, the guard from Vinney Green would be quick to reassure him and ask if he was OK.

He would nod then and I'd feel a wave of anger rise inside me. What about *us*? No one asked us if *we* were OK! In fact, on that day, I felt really alone. John and Charmaine weren't present and though we were briefly introduced to another officer called Carol Saunders, I didn't really have a clue what was going on. I didn't even know where we were supposed to sit, and had to ask someone from Witness Care, who could only tell us that someone would run through everything with us afterwards – so during the hearing itself I just felt totally bewildered.

Most of what was said that day in court is still a blur. All I recall was first hearing the date read out – Becca's birth date – and then the charge: 'for the murder of Rebecca Aylward'. It was almost as if I'd been hit by a bolt of lightning – the shock and horror of it all seemed to hit me like a solid physical force. All I could think of was how I could make it over to the dock before any of the court officials could stop me. I wanted to kill him; I wanted so much to kill him in that moment that I began to feel frightened I'd actually do it.

It took a huge effort of will to remain in my seat that day. I just had to keep telling myself over and over that I must do absolutely nothing to jeopardise the case. I must not be in contempt of court before the trial even started. And I wanted to be there – I wanted to see him squirm on that stand. I wanted – needed – to see him go down. Perhaps I would have my chance then.

CHAPTER FIFTEEN

MILESTONES

After the court hearing on Becca's birthday, a hearing at the Old Bailey was quickly scheduled. On 4 March 2011, at the Central Criminal Court (as the Old Bailey is officially known), the judge and barristers gathered for their pre-trial review. Davies wasn't present and neither was I: this was a hearing to determine when the case itself would come to court.

Everyone, I imagine, has heard of the Old Bailey in London and, as a family, we were no exception. Becca and I had even talked about it, more than once.

Becca had been just eight when she had decided on her chosen career ambition to become a barrister. And within that ambition she had another, which she shared with me one day while we were having one of our usual lengthy chats.

'Just think, Mam,' she'd said excitedly while Jess sat and played with her Barbies. 'That could be me, couldn't it? If I work hard, I could be working at the Old Bailey one day!'

I didn't doubt for a moment that she'd do it. And as a prosecutor, because that had always been Becca's goal: to be instrumental in getting justice for the victims. How awful it felt – how wretchedly ironic – that she would now appear there, not as counsel for the prosecution, as she had so often dreamed about, but as a name read out in court: as a victim herself.

The judge was apparently keen that they move quickly. It was noted in court that our family had already suffered enough and a provisional trial date of 21 March was suggested. But it was not to be: the defence team maintained that it was necessary to delay things as they'd had insufficient time to go through the evidence.

I had my own feelings about that and, to some extent, it reassured me. At that point, I knew that their line of defence – their only one – was that it had been Ninnis, not Davies, who had killed Becca. But what I also knew, both from the evidence I'd handed over and from what the police had always told me, was that the evidence stacking up against Davies was indefensible.

There was another factor that had to be taken into consideration, though. It was that Becca's friends all had GCSE exams to face and having the trial happening before then would disrupt their revision. Though I understood the reasons for the delay and accepted that it was right to let Becca's friends – some of whom would be called as witnesses – get their exams over with, it felt like a huge blow, another enormous emotional hurdle to clamber over. Having tried to prepare myself for what I knew would be a massive ordeal (I had no idea how I'd manage to sit in court day after day, having to relive the horror of what had been done to my daughter), I felt this overwhelming sense of letdown that it was now not going to happen. More than ever, time seemed to stand still.

In so many ways, I wanted everything to move faster; to rush by in a blur so I didn't have to dwell on all the horrible milestones Jack, Jess and I had to endure.

Mother's Day came around, much as I'd tried to blank it from my mind, and it was as bad as I'd known it would be. The children had always made a fuss of me on Mothering Sunday, creating little video messages, which would always have me in tears, and lovely handmade cards. And since Jack had been tiny, Becca – being the eldest and so thoughtful – would always sit and help him make his card for me.

Jack and Jess, bless their hearts, both made me cards and gave me gifts but, much as I treasured them, the day was just so painful.

Hard on its heels came another milestone – my 50th birthday. We had talked about it often and, Becca being Becca, she had already started making plans for it before she was taken from us, telling me how she planned to track down everyone – even far-flung relatives and old school friends I'd not seen in years – and make sure they could come to my party. But again, it wasn't to be. Instead, my birthday gift was to be a witness at her murder trial and, after what seemed like ages, as each day seemed interminable, I finally had a letter from Witness Care, the branch of the Crown Prosecution Service whose job it was to take care of us, explain what we had to do in court as witnesses, and keep us informed about the progress of the trial. The trial itself was now scheduled to go ahead on 20 June 2011 – which still seemed half a lifetime away. The thought of building myself up all over again was mentally exhausting; I wasn't even sure how I'd be able to go through with it.

But again, I felt Becca driving me to get justice for her so, once more, I started to prepare myself for what I would have to see and hear in court. I became focused then – focused on the one thing that mattered more to me than almost anything else: finding out *what* had happened and, even more importantly, finding out *why* it had happened and getting the monster who'd murdered my daughter locked away for good.

As spring progressed, full of sunshine and warmth and longer days, the contrast between the coming of summer and the nightmare we were living through seemed to intensify. Every day I woke up and expected to be released from it and then my conscious mind would suddenly kick in and remind me that there *was* no waking up from it: this was it, she had gone. We would have to feel like this every single morning for the rest of our lives.

Becca had so been looking forward to the summer that was burgeoning all around us. She'd said it several times the previous autumn. The previous year she'd had such a miserable summer and the reasons for it had completely baffled everyone.

She had started becoming ill at the beginning of the year, shortly after having split up from Davies. For some reason she'd begun to feel constantly nauseous and, more scarily, she'd started having dizzy spells too. And we had no idea why: she'd always been such a healthy child and teenager but now she was feeling ill all the time.

I was frightened. It didn't seen normal for a young healthy person to be having blackouts and, when I took her to the GP surgery, the doctor agreed with me and said she would refer her to a specialist.

Becca was referred to the hospital in the February of the previous year and began having investigations to try and work out what might be wrong with her. And it seemed such a mystery to everyone. Initially, there was some talk of it perhaps being psychological, as we had all been going through such a stressful time in relation to my ex-husband, but for me that just didn't ring true. You know your own children and it just didn't seem to fit with how Becca was in herself generally, although as the months went by and each different medical test came back negative, I was becoming increasingly baffled.

Linda's and my biggest fear was that she had a brain tumour and so, when her MRI scan was returned normal, we were greatly relieved. But still no one had any idea what could be the cause of the blackouts, which by late summer were becoming more frequent. There seemed to be no pattern to them either. One day, Linda was driving Becca into town to take her shopping when she told her she felt very strange. 'I feel odd,' she said to Linda. 'You know – weird. As if I'm not myself.'

'OK,' Linda said, 'I'll pull in as soon as I can.'

But Becca, who had her head resting against the car window at the time, didn't reply.

'*Becca?*' Linda said, frantically looking for a place where she could pull in safely. '*Becca?*' she said again, this time giving her a gentle shake as well. But it was only on the third occasion that Becca finally stirred. She turned and looked at Linda just as she was pulling in to the side of the road. 'Are you OK?' Linda asked her, seeing how pale and strange she looked. 'Did you faint?'

'I don't know,' Becca told her. 'I just suddenly felt so woozy.'

She had no idea that she'd actually blacked out for a full two minutes.

I was becoming sick with worry now – what if next time it happened somewhere dangerous – when Becca was alone, say, or in the middle of crossing a road? The consultant paediatrician promised me she'd conduct some more tests but only a fortnight later, at the beginning of September, it happened again.

I was in my bedroom on that occasion and Becca was in the bathroom next door when I heard this really loud crash through the wall. I rushed to the bathroom door and banged on it several times but without any response.

'Are you OK?' I shouted. Again nothing. I pressed my ear to the door. '*Becca!*' I called again, panicking, as it had, by now, been a good half-minute. 'Are you OK in there? Can you hear me? Can you call to me? Because if I don't hear something soon, I'm going to have to bash down the door!' And I would have as well, except, just at the point when I was going to rush downstairs and get something to do it with, I heard her blearily asking me what for.

'*Becca!*' I called again. 'Are you awake now? Are you OK? Can you let me in?'

She looked dreadful – ill and shaky, confused and also deathly pale. She'd obviously fallen heavily too, as she was clearly in pain. 'What happened?' I asked her, sitting her down on the side of the bath and putting my arm around her to steady her.

'I don't know,' she said. 'I was just lying on the floor and heard you knocking – I don't have any idea how I got there.'

This was becoming truly frightening and once again I rushed

her straight to the doctors but, apart from taking her blood pressure and temperature, and checking her reflexes and responses, there wasn't a great deal they could do. She was obviously still under the care of her consultant at the hospital and awaiting the results of various tests. 'Just keep a close eye on her,' was the only help they could offer.

And by the next appointment at the hospital, it had happened a further couple of times, with her once falling against her bedroom door, blocking my entry, and once I'd got to her – through the connecting door shared with Jess's bedroom – telling me that she'd seen white spots before her eyes prior to passing out.

I was almost out of my mind worrying about what might be wrong with her by now and, although I still felt reassured by the fact that the MRI scan hadn't picked up anything on her brain, I couldn't quite accept that it could be anything other than serious. Yet nothing the doctors tried seemed to get to the heart of it. She had endless blood tests – which were incredibly painful as she had inherited such tiny veins – as well as 24-hour heart monitoring, neurophysiological investigations and, at the beginning of October, various tests for sleep deprivation, in which numerous wires were glued all over her head, ruining the hair she'd straightened only that morning.

'I'm so fed up with this,' she'd told me as we were in the hospital toilets, trying to get the glue out. 'Look at the state of me – I can't go outside like this!'

And all of it – all the inconvenience, all the stress, all the pain, all the missed schooling – for nothing: she was dead before the results even came through.

Right now, I was worried about my two younger children. My beautiful little family was now so horribly fractured and I feared for what would happen to Jessica and Jack. Becca had always been so close to them – always so much a little mum to them – and I was so frightened about how they'd cope once the time came for them to return to school. How would they get over this? How would they ever manage to get back to their education? When would they have the strength to return to any version of normality?

We had talked for a long time, Jessica and I, about her returning to Archbishop McGrath and, though she tried going back in May, it soon became clear that it wasn't going to be workable. How could it be, really?

Liam Thomas had never been arrested and at this point all I knew of his involvement was that he'd been with Davies and Ninnis in the café on the morning of Becca's death and that it had been he who Davies had contacted via his mobile to tell him and Ninnis to join him up in the woods. He was now, of course, back in school as normal, getting on with his life.

And as if that wasn't upsetting enough for Jess, there was also the matter of Daniel Ninnis, who *had* been arrested along with Davies. He'd been released without charge very swiftly by the police, who were in no doubt that it had been Davies who'd actually done the deed. But it was still so hard for her to face him.

Ninnis might have been released but he was still part of the ongoing investigation and the thought of him being on the same school premises as Jessica appalled me. No wonder, given that he had been present at the scene where her sister had been murdered, that he still frightened Jessica. No wonder, therefore, that the last thing I wanted was her back at that place every day, having to face him.

There was also the fact that I kept coming back to – that one of Davies's younger brothers, Jordan, was in the school, as was Tyler Harry. How could Jessica deal with seeing those boys every day, knowing what their brother had done to her sister? It was intolerable for her: intolerable and terrifying. And, although she tried, she soon realised she couldn't stay there as well, and we arranged for her to transfer to Maesteg Comprehensive, at least until Ninnis and Thomas left school..

I knew I had less of a worry about Jack, which was a small comfort, at least, because he was still at his primary school, St Mary's and St Patrick's and had settled back in after Christmas. They were wonderful in every respect. The teachers were all so kind, particularly his class teacher, Miss Maria Browne, who had already shown such incredible thoughtfulness and kindness, right from the time of Becca's murder. She'd been amazing, coming round with home-baked biscuits and cakes so that, when people came round – from the police to our family to Becca's school friends – we could offer them with cups of tea. She also brought vases, something which at the time, in my befuddled state, I couldn't understand but, of course, they were receptacles for the many flowers that were sent to us; no one household could ever have owned enough.

Maria Browne had also come one day with a cuddly toy called Miss Sunshine and instructed the children that Miss Sunshine had a very important role to play – they had to hug her every time they thought of Becca. She had taught all of my children at some point and I knew Jack would be in a pair of safe, loving hands when once again entrusted to her and her colleagues' care. And once we'd set a date for his return, just after Christmas, I went into school to see her personally, to explain about the coming trial and what was going to happen.

'Don't worry about him at *all*,' she reassured me. 'We'll be like another family for him. You can trust us, Sonia – we won't let you down.'

And she didn't – she would go on to look after him so well during the gruelling weeks ahead and I owe her a huge debt of gratitude.

There was to be no open-armed, safe, loving return for Jessica, however. At the end of May she had no choice but to officially leave her faith school, not to mention all her friends and everything that was familiar, and go to join her new school in Maesteg. They were wonderful at the school and I couldn't thank them enough – I still can't – because they welcomed her at a time of great personal tragedy and the staff took incredibly good care of her. She would be safe there, they promised me, and I trusted that she would but, at the same time, I felt sick with nerves on her behalf. It's bad enough for any teenager to be wrenched away from everything they know and love but, in Jessica's case, it must have felt like a mountain she had to climb; was already climbing, through an impenetrable fog of grief. It was a time when she really needed the support of her familiar Catholic school 'family', yet she – the victim's sister and so a victim herself – was the one who had to be removed and taken away from all her friends.

I had tried my best to stop this happening, as it just seemed so incredibly unfair. As well as sending endless emails questioning why it wasn't at least Ninnis who was expected to move schools, I had numerous meetings and conversations with both the Head and the Priest-governor but all they could do was reassure me that she'd be safe where she was.

But I didn't believe them. Had Becca been safe while she'd been there? Clearly not! And though it would be the trial itself before I heard evidence that would corroborate that point dramatically, in the meantime, it was my choice to make. It didn't seem to matter that she'd be terrified, constantly looking over her shoulder, walking into a place that held her sister's murderer's friends and relatives.

And if I'd hoped the parents of Thomas or Ninnis would remove their own children (or, at the very least, get them home tutors temporarily), it was destined to be a vain hope, so I didn't even go there. No, it was Jessica who must continue to suffer as a result of her sister's murder – Jessica alone – and go to a place where she barely knew a soul.

But it wasn't just the spectre of those boys that upset me: there was also the unwelcome attention that Jess and Jack were likely to receive from their peers, day to day. Of course some of it would be well-meaning and I knew their friends would try and protect them but some would just be idle curiosity. It seemed so cruel and so unfair that they should have to carry such a huge burden at so young an age.

I was shocked by just how little there was in terms of help and support, given how much they had had to endure, not to mention the life-sentence of pain they had ahead of them and the terrible loss of the big sister who'd always helped and guided them. So it was left for me to try and somehow know the right way to handle things when I could barely function myself. But handle it I would; I could hear Becca telling me I had to and if I didn't, I knew I'd feel I'd failed her. And it was a help, something to focus on, a job that needed doing, as at some point soon it would be important that they did both return to school and begin the slow process of trying to rebuild their lives.

I explained to them, just as the police had explained to me, that they should remember that Davies was a liar. He had lied – and been found out – but it was important that they remember that there would continue to be lies told about everything. And what they needed to do was shut their ears to it and walk away. I told them I was the only one who knew the truth about what had happened and I promised them that, when the time was right – which wasn't yet – I would tell them all of it.

I also knew that I needed to protect Jack and Jessica from the media. Though we were mostly left alone by now, I knew that state of affairs was temporary. As soon as the trial began, it would again be splashed all over the papers and also – because I had watched enough TV in my life to know it – in a case such as this, there would be endless news bulletins, as the details of what happened began to come out in court.

The police, as with everything, were brilliant. They told the press that I promised that I would speak to them at length just as soon as the trial was over and I'm sure they were instrumental in ensuring that the media respected our wishes and let us try to grieve and come to terms with everything left well alone.

If I was worried about the questions Jack and Jessica would be bombarded with from friends, I was terrified of what they might hear and read in the press. I knew so little of what had happened but they knew even less. And that was how I wanted it; I was braced to listen to whatever horrors I had to listen to because I had to, for Becca, but I didn't want that for her little brother and sister – I didn't want all that evil and brutality spelled out to them because their young minds, I knew, would be unable to cope. And they had more than enough to cope with already.

Towards the end of May, Witness Care got in touch with me again to say that the trial would definitely commence on 20 June 2011, in Swansea Crown Court. By now, the police seemed to be in touch with me almost daily – checking and rechecking every detail about everything, and asking endless questions about names and whether I had heard of them.

It was a constant quest for details and I felt reassured they were doing absolutely everything in their power to leave nothing to chance. One detail in particular was the nail varnish Becca had been wearing that fateful day. They'd asked about it often and, as previously mentioned, had already taken away all her nail varnishes, although, of course, they hadn't told me why it was so important. And then, one day, an important memory came to me out of the blue: they hadn't had *all* her nail varnishes after all.

I don't know why it hit me when it did but, once it did, it all made sense; I also knew I'd recalled something very important. I remembered that on the Friday, the night before Becca was murdered, she and Jess had been doing their nails together downstairs in the living room. Becca had painted Jess's nails in the same pink as hers and I now recalled what Jess had said to me a few days after the murder; that she never wanted to paint over her nails again.

I must have taken it in at the time but in the midst of my grief perhaps only subconsciously. And now I had remembered it consciously and I knew it was the key to the whereabouts of that crucial bottle of nail varnish. Yes, I'd given the police what I'd *thought* were all Becca's bottles but this one had been missing because they'd done their nails downstairs.

All those bottles they'd taken months back to be sent away for testing and the very one that they needed had still been here all along. I ran downstairs and, sure enough, there it was, up on the bookshelf, exactly where Becca must have left it. I called Charmaine and told her; she came straight round to collect it. And once I'd signed her paperwork, as I had to with everything I handed over, she sent it straight down to London for testing.

I wouldn't know the results, of course, but I knew from the way Charmaine had been so pleased I'd found it that it was a vital piece of physical evidence. Already I knew Becca's nail varnish must matter because I knew they'd bagged her hands to preserve evidence. Was this the single most important thing the prosecution had?

I wouldn't know till the trial but I knew that was the way it had to be. They were being incredibly careful to do everything by the book because it would take only the tiniest lapse in following the correct protocol for Davies's lawyers to have grounds for appeal.

I had found this hard at first, this need to be slightly excluded, as I'd seen it, but now I no longer cared. Davies must be treated fairly, presumed innocent until conclusively proven guilty so that, once he *was* found guilty – and I trusted the police's assurance that he would be – it would be both beyond reasonable doubt and incontrovertible. And then I would finally see justice done.

Though I had, by now, accepted that my million questions were not going to be answered till the trial itself began, and that I had to leave the police to get on with their jobs, there was, at least, something I could do to help the case. As both Linda and I were witnesses and would be giving evidence in court, Charmaine suggested that we might like to make a visit to Court Number 1, where all serious cases were heard.

Ross, from Victim Support, agreed. 'It might help a lot,' he told us when I spoke to him on the phone to arrange it. 'It can be extremely daunting being a witness in a Crown Court – very intimidating. So if you familiarise yourselves beforehand, you won't feel quite so nervous on the day.'

I did not want to feel *anything* on the day that might make me mess up being cross-examined, so a few days later, on a quiet court day, Linda drove Jess and me to Swansea so we could see for ourselves the place where Linda and I were going to give our evidence and the same for Jess, assuming she was called as well. Jack, thank goodness, was once again too young.

Swansea actually has two Crown Courts, which sit across the road from each other. One of them is the original building and is imposing and traditional in style, and the other – Court Number 1, where Davies's trial would take place, was newer. I was a little disappointed by the look of it – it reminded me of a block of ordinary offices – but once we got inside, my view quickly changed.

I had never seen the inside of a Crown Court before and, once we were standing in it, the 'office' likeness disappeared in a stroke. It was a court of law and I found it overwhelming. It was nothing like the magistrates court where I'd sat and faced Davies before and I felt a wave of self-doubt rise inside me as soon as we entered. Could I even do this without cracking up?

At the invitation of the usher who was accompanying the three of us and Ross, I went and stood in the witness box, where I'd be standing to give my evidence, suddenly all too aware that all eyes would be on me, from Davies himself to the jury to the two rows of legal teams to the press; that when I spoke, *everyone* in the court would be looking right at me. It was a frightening thought.

I looked across at the dock then, which was surrounded by glass. It was obviously there to protect whoever was standing in it from any rougher kind of justice and I imagined Davies standing behind it in his neatly pressed trousers, trying to create the impression that he was a vulnerable, innocent lad. How would *he* react when he had no choice but to face me? To finally have to listen to me giving evidence against him; having to squirm under my scrutiny, knowing that I knew the truth? I would be doing it while looking him straight in the eye too, wishing him dead. I'd never felt anything quite so strongly in my life.

It was something I had never, ever expected to feel either. But then before our world fell apart, I could never have imagined what it would be like to lose my own child, to lose a life I had created inside me and nurtured – a new human being, to whom it was my job to teach right from wrong.

It was a job I relished. I was a Christian and always will be; I believed in God before Becca was taken from me and I believe in him now. It's a huge source of comfort in a life that's been so blighted. I brought up my children to believe in Christianity as well; to know the importance of family and to help others less fortunate than themselves, which is why I was so glad they went to the primary school they did because they did such a good job there of instilling that as well.

My children loved their primary school, and so did I, and supporting them was one of the things that made me happiest – to find things for their auctions, to help out at the school fête. Anything we could do as a family to help we always did because something else Christianity taught me – and I know I instilled that in my children – was that helping others also made you feel better about yourself.

I never in all my life hated anyone or wished them dead and to have this much hatred to carry around was exhausting. It also broke my heart to know that the very qualities I instilled in my children were the ones that made Becca always try to see the good in the monster who had killed her. That was what she did – always tried to see the other person's point of view – and, with Davies, particularly when she knew he was struggling with his studies, all she wanted to do was try to help him. And she continued to do this even when he was nasty to her. So hard-wired to try and see the good in every person, she would just tell herself he must be joking.

Seeing evil at work at such close quarters changes a person. Where once I only saw good, now the first thing I would ever see was bad; comparing everyone to Davies, to his mannerisms, to his scheming and to his lies. Going from a place where you trust everyone to having no faith in humanity is a life sentence in itself.

The judge's chair in Court Number 1 sat at the centre of everything; it was from here that the accumulated wisdom of centuries would, I prayed, see justice was dispensed. I imagined the judge himself sitting there, an intimidating and towering presence, and I realised that, for all the anxiety that was building inside me, I had faith. I believed in him or her; I trusted their wisdom, trusted that they would see to it that justice *was* done here.

But it wasn't just down to the judge, of course. There would also be a jury of twelve men and women, who would be sitting in the two rows of seats to the judge's right. I looked at the empty spaces and tried to imagine them filled with strangers. *Oh, God*, I thought, *who* were *they? Had they already been chosen? And what sort of people would they be? Did they have children too? Please*, I thought, *please let them be parents, like me. Please let them see through Davies's mask of innocence, through his cleverness at lying, his skill at manipulating people, and straight to the evil psychopath that lay underneath.*

Thinking of Davies standing in that very court actually made me feel better. Because if it was intimidating for me now, what would it be like for him? How would he feel, stepping into this room – this Crown Court for serious offences? I hoped he would falter, that he would crack up and fall apart.

'That was a good idea,' I told Linda as Ross finally led us out. Though I had been shaken by it and now felt extremely anxious about what was coming, it had been useful because it had made me realise how important it was that I now pull myself together; I had to do this for Becca, to make sure that justice was done. To make sure Davies was locked up for what he'd done to my baby.

There was still a great deal I didn't know but one thing I *did* know was that Davies had been talking about killing Becca. And those boys had heard him talking about it, even if they had thought it was all a big joke. They had still heard him, and by their own admission they had told nobody.

Both boys were now going to be called as witnesses for the prosecution, however – something that was apparently vital if we were to get a murder conviction.

A conviction I wanted more than anything now. I was beginning to count the days.

PART THREE

PART THREE

CHAPTER SIXTEEN

CROWN COURT

Monday, 20 June 2011

On the day that I first arrived in Swansea Crown Court for the trial of my daughter's murder, it had been eight months, almost to the day, since she had been taken from me. And in all that time, I had learned almost nothing about her killing. I knew *what* had happened – she had been killed after several violent blows to the back of her skull – and I knew who had done it too: without question, Joshua Davies. But I still had no idea what chain of events had led to that moment. What could possibly have happened? I needed answers like I needed air to breathe.

I had spent the previous two weeks in a frenzy of anxiety and organisation. As the trial loomed, I became increasingly fearful about the verdict. Though I had no shred of doubt about Davies having been Becca's murderer, I had no idea how strong the prosecution case actually was. I knew they had lots of anecdotal evidence, not to mention the testimonies of Ninnis and Thomas, but with their conflicting stories, I knew we were also dealing with lies. Did the prosecution have enough actual physical evidence alone to convict Davies? I was worried because John Doherty had told me that some of the forensic results were still not back yet; I didn't know what they were, only that the police were concerned about them. And suppose they didn't get back in time? Suppose they were the ones that were crucial to getting that conviction? Perhaps they had become contaminated, or been lost along the way?

I didn't know a great deal about the law but I knew barristers were very skilful and that Davies would have a defence team who would be determined to get him acquitted. Suppose they did? What *then*? It was then that I realised why Becca was so determined she'd never do that sort of defence work – because in some cases there was no doubt and it was about finding some technicality so that a murderer could be set free to walk the streets.

I was so fearful that it had been cathartic to be so busy in the days leading to the trial. There had been an incredible amount to organise because it would, effectively, take over six weeks of all our family's lives. Jess would be coming to court with me every day, just in case she was called to give evidence, but Jack wouldn't, so I had to liaise with his school as well as arrange before- and after-school childcare for him while we were in court every day.

I also had to shop for enough food that we didn't have to constantly be out and about getting supplies. In fact, I really had to think of it as being under siege. I knew full well that, as soon as proceedings commenced, we'd be back in the spotlight again because the press would be following the trial every day and reporting back to their various newspapers and television and radio shows. I'd sat and watched such things myself, after all – all those reporters stood outside court clutching their microphones, talking to the camera, sharing the most salacious and riveting developments in a case as they emerged.

Only now it would be my family and me under the spotlight. Would the paparazzi try to get shots of us? Would journalists actually follow us around, trying to get comments? I didn't know quite what to expect, only that it was an extra pressure at a time when we were physically and mentally exhausted, but we could do nothing about it so we planned for the worst. Linda and I had left no stone unturned. We had planned our route to court carefully and sorted out parking. The latter was a huge problem at Swansea Crown Court, apparently, and once again, if we didn't find a way to do so easily then we'd be bombarded by the media every single day of the trial.

And that was exactly what happened on day one. I had hardly slept the night before and, by the time I arrived at the court at 8.30am, flanked by Linda, Roger and Janet, I felt so anxious and nauseous that a couple of times I almost made a dash for the ladies', thinking I was about to throw up. I had also brought sunglasses with me – not because of the brightness of the summer morning, but because I knew I'd probably break down and would have permanently puffy eyes. Funny the things that come to you but I was just so aware of all the press being present and how they would probably be constantly taking photos of us. And I'd been right: as well as all the police officers, there were journalists and cameramen and women *everywhere*. There were even more than I'd imagined and, as my family bundled me – almost literally – through the huge throng of people towards the entrance, the only thing that kept my knees from buckling under me was the thought of Becca, close beside me, willing me to keep going and promising me I would soon see justice done.

We went into the court through a big entrance, in front of which there was a lay-by, currently cordoned off by tape, to stop anybody parking there. The door was guarded by two big burly-looking police officers and, as soon as we passed them, we had to go through a scanner and also be scanned with a hand-held one, like they have at airports. It was sobering to think that we were in a place where criminals were routinely present; how many murderers, rapists, arsonists and bank robbers had been through this same process we were now going through?

We were then met by a friendly face; a lady called Lorraine, who told us she'd be looking after us and took us upstairs to a room, close to Court 1, which had a sign saying 'Oatley family' stuck to the door. As was by now becoming usual (and surprising, as I had previously been such a quiet person), I began bombarding her with questions. And chief among them, perhaps naturally, was 'where will his family be?'

Lorraine showed us another room, even closer to the court itself, which, unlike ours, had glass panels that gave onto the inside of the building, so that the people outside could see in. I didn't know what the reason for this was but it seemed appropriate: it meant everyone could look into the room where the Davies family gathered, whereas we had complete privacy.

Our own room, which was opposite the room where Lorraine told us they stored items of physical evidence, had windows on the outside, which looked down over the front of the building. As I looked out, I could see that a large car had pulled up in the previously cordoned-off lay-by, out of which were climbing a number of officers I recognised as being from the Major Crimes Unit. One had opened the boot and I was just about to ask Lorraine what they were doing when I saw for myself.

I must have gasped because Lorraine immediately came to my side and asked me if I was OK. I was transfixed, though, seeing all the brown bags they were unloading from the car because I could make out what was in most of them from the shapes. I saw what looked like laptops, mobile phones and other bags that obviously contained clothes and, as another bag came out with what looked like spade handles sticking out of it, my mind started to whirr into overdrive. *Oh, my God*, I thought. *What were* they *used for? To hit her? To try and bury her?* What had happened that day that I didn't know about? All that time and I'd believed it had just been one blow that had killed her. What had *really* happened? What hadn't they told me? Anger boiled in me, so much so that I had a powerful violent urge to run into the Davies family's room and throttle his mother with my bare hands for creating such a monster, such pure evil.

I felt Linda's arm on mine, warm and firm. 'Come on,' she said, leading me away. 'Come and sit down. And *calm* down, OK, Son? Calm *down!*'

She was right, of course. I'd be no use to Becca if I kept getting in such a state. This was what I knew was going to happen, wasn't it? That I'd hear things and see things that I didn't want to see or hear, however much I'd been desperate for answers. So I sat but it was a real effort of will to do so and I knew it would continue to be until I could get into court and listen for myself.

The first morning was mostly taken up with formalities. First, the jury had to be sworn in and then there would be opening speeches from both the prosecution and defence barristers. It was only after they were done that an usher came back into the room to tell us that Roger and Janet needed to take their places in court.

I felt my stomach heave, watching them silently stand up and leave the room. Linda and I wouldn't be able to go with them, of course, because we were both witnesses for the prosecution. We wouldn't be able to be present until we'd given our own evidence, so it was up to Roger and Janet to be our eyes and ears instead. They might not be able to tell us anything yet but I still wanted them there to hear it so that, once they could sit down and share it with me, they would be able to.

Once they'd gone, however, I couldn't settle again and was back to pacing the room and clock watching. Linda, once again, came to my rescue. 'Come on,' she said, 'let's get out of here. Let's go down to the café and get a coffee,' taking my arm and leading me out of the room even as she was suggesting it.

The café was back downstairs and, on our way there, we passed another waiting room. Through the open door I could see other anxious families. *Why?* I thought, seeing the tension and worry on their faces. *Why was the world so cruel? Why did we have to endure such torment?*

The café was all but empty and I was thankful. There was no press there to badger me or people to offer condolences and sympathy – much as I was grateful for sympathy, I didn't want to see it in people's faces; it just reminded me that all I really wanted was not to be here at all, to go back in time, to a time when I still had Becca. I was in such a state of tension by now that I couldn't even do something as simple as order a coffee but, as ever, Linda was by my side, endlessly supportive, sitting me down as if I were a child and she was my mother, taking care of me, being so strong. And all the while, I knew, suffering every bit as much as I was. I really don't know how I would have coped without her.

We sat and drank our coffee and discussed what might be happening upstairs but, when barristers began coming into the café in some numbers, we realised we must say nothing more in such a public place because some of them might be Davies's defence counsel. Feeling unable to stay, we then made our way back up to our waiting room again, where, at 11.30am, Roger and Janet finally returned, their faces pale, their expressions like stone.

'*What?*' I asked my brother, shocked by how distraught he looked. 'What have they said in there? *What?*'

He couldn't tell me, of course; he could only reassure me that he'd heard nothing I hadn't already been told by the police. 'It just hits you so hard,' he explained, shaking his head. 'Sitting there listening to the barristers describing everything so openly and clinically. It just really hits you, Son. You are going to need to brace yourself, OK?'

Tuesday, 21 June 2011

I had spent a sleepless night going over and over everything I might be asked about and, my mind still in overdrive, spent several hours searching everything I could find in case there was anything I might have missed. I went through every single school book I could find, just in case there was something incriminating in one of them, remembering the contrast between Becca, who kept everything so neat and tidy, and the seeming compulsion Davies appeared to have to break and spoil things. There had been many occasions when he'd deface one of her school books, usually with some crude or cruel comment about someone or other. She'd also come home from school with pens and pencils in her pencil case snapped in half. 'How did that happen?' I would ask. 'Oh, that was Josh,' she'd reply. It was as if he had a compulsion to destroy.

But I had the rest of my life to grieve and feel angry; right now I must keep a sense of focus and purpose. Take care of Jack and Jessica, make sure they were fed and rested, tell them as much as I felt was appropriate and prepare myself for whatever the next day would bring, hoping that, as I became used to the routine, each day would be just that little bit easier. However, it wasn't long into the morning of the second day in court before I realised that might not happen; that every day was going to be as difficult as the one before it. That after so many months in my bubble of pain and grief, I was now going to have to stare what had happened in the face, including the faces of all the people who had been involved.

I was to find that out immediately, in fact. I was waiting to hear from Jill, the court usher, what the order of events for the second day would be when I looked out of the window to find myself staring straight at Liam Thomas, the boy who had finally told his mother what had happened to Becca and whose father had been the one to call the police. I'd heard many rumours about what he knew from Becca's friends – who he was obviously still in school with – but very little as yet from the police.

He was sitting on the wall below us with another witness I recognised – a boy called Dan Carter, who I'd never actually met but recognised from photos Becca had shown me. Catching my eye and realising who I was, Liam Thomas immediately looked away. But I continued to glare at him, so his next glance upwards found him looking into my eyes once again, whereupon I saw him mouth the words 'Becca's mother', as his friend Don Carter had obviously asked who I was.

It really hit me then how hard a job it would be to hold it together over the coming weeks because just watching those lips say the name of my daughter made me want to rush down there and tell him what I thought of him. And I think I might have done so, had Linda not been there to stop me.

Fortunately, Lorraine came back into the room soon after, giving us all something to focus on at last. But as soon as she started speaking – running through the order of the day's events – it became clear I had another fight on my hands. At that point I didn't really know anything about how court cases were organised, obviously, but had naturally already formed an idea. Now that the opening addresses by the prosecution and defence counsels had been dealt with, I knew it would be a question of the prosecution calling witnesses to the stand. And I assumed that they would do so roughly in an order that matched up to the sequence of events.

This wasn't just ill-informed supposition either, it had always made sense to me because, as John Doherty had already explained (as had Ross from Victim Support, who'd shown us round the court, back in May), the jury would need to be told a kind of 'story' of events, so they could make sense of everything that had happened. It had therefore seemed natural to assume that Linda and I would be called fairly early, since it was us who had first raised the alarm. But it turned out I was wrong. When Lorraine ran through the order in which witnesses were going to be called, it seemed that Linda and I were some way down the list.

Liam Thomas's mother, Paula – another person who had never sent a card or message of condolence – would be called to the witness box first that morning, Lorraine explained, to give her evidence about the sequence of events after Liam told her what had happened. After she'd spoken, there would be statements from the officers who'd taken part in the search for Becca and then from several of Becca and Davies's school friends. And after all that had been done, Daniel Ninnis and Liam Thomas would be called.

It took a few moments for this to sink in. I had no idea how long all these elements would take. A day? Two days? A week? It seemed such a long time. But one thing hit me with such force that it was like a physical assault – that, if that were the case, I wouldn't be able to be in court to sit and listen to either Ninnis or Thomas give their evidence.

I wasn't stupid; I was a witness and I understood what that meant for me. I'd lived through being kept out of the loop for many months now and I understood why that needed to be so. But what I couldn't contemplate was the thought that, having finally got to the trial, I wouldn't be able to be in court for the two testimonies – after Davies taking the stand, of course – that I most wanted and needed to hear. These boys were key witnesses to the crime. There was no way they could give evidence without me there.

'*No!*' I said to Lorraine, mortified. 'It can't happen that way!'

I don't know where I found the strength of mind that morning but find it I did. It was unthinkable that they should give their evidence and that I wouldn't be allowed to be there to hear it. And that gave me the strength to find the wherewithal to fight. I didn't care about Thomas's mother, or the testimony of the various school friends, but I needed to give my evidence before those boys – I also felt I had a right to – and I wasn't going to take no for an answer.

And I got my way. By mid-morning I was called out of our room and told that the prosecution barrister, Gregg Taylor QC, had agreed to move things around so that I could give my evidence first, so that I could then attend court and finally sit and watch proceedings – the very next morning, in fact.

The obvious relief I felt at this development came with a side order of yet more fear. As the reality kicked in that I was soon to take the stand, I felt like a terrified child facing an exam. And for the first time since the day he had taken my child from me, thoughts of Davies didn't occupy my head. All I could think of was that I must remember every detail, must remember to look at the jury as I spoke, as I'd been told to, must remember to answer every question calmly and accurately.

It would be a tall order at any time but particularly so, given my fragile emotional state. But if there was one comfort, it was my confidence that, however difficult it proved to be, Becca would be beside me, willing me on.

Wednesday, 22 June 2011

I was to be the second witness called on the third day of the trial, after a boy called Josh Perkins and a number of Becca's other friends. Again, I didn't know anything about the content of their statements but I did know – because so many of them had already told me personally – that Davies had told all sorts of people of his plans to kill Becca.

I was very well supported. Both Roger and Janet had come again, plus my two Lorraines: Lorraine Surringer, Becca's wonderful English teacher and, coincidentally, a distant relative, and one of my dearest friends (and Janet's sister), Lorraine Williams. But as I watched my family file out of the room and back into the court after the first break, my head was still all over the place. On the one hand, I was desperate to get in there and get it over with, but at the same time I was dreading what was coming after that. Once I'd done what I had to do, I would be in there day after day, having to listen – and in great detail – to the events that led to my daughter's final moments on this earth. I couldn't get that picture out of my head; that image of her happy smile as she got ready that Saturday morning, little knowing she was about to meet the Devil himself, that it would be that last time I would ever see her.

I tried deep breaths as a means to stop my heart thumping in my chest and my stomach from churning over and over. I had tried to memorise everything – and when you are telling the truth, that's not so difficult – but was terrified it would all come out wrong; that I'd get muddled about the times of all the phone calls and texts, that the pressure of all those questions and all those jurors looking at me would make my brain jumble everything up.

And the longer I waited, the more the contents of my memory seemed to scramble, so I was almost relieved when the door opened and Jill, the court usher, was in the doorway. 'They're ready for you now, Sonia,' she said.

I followed her up to the courtroom, passing several barristers, who were all rushing to and fro and, as we stood outside the double swing doors waiting for the signal that we could enter, I wondered whether the judge would have already told everyone who I was. Would he have explained to them, or would they know nothing about me till my name was called? I could see the judge straight ahead and the public gallery to my right, where my family and Davies's family sat, so incredibly close.

'I call Sonia Aylward!' called Gregg Taylor QC, upon which Jill opened the door and I followed her in.

It's a cliché but I did feel as if I was in a goldfish bowl. I could feel everyone's eyes on me as I made my way across the echoing wooden floor to the witness stand. *Be strong*, I kept telling myself. *Don't break down and cry. Keep yourself together. You must stay strong.*

I'd been told it was important that I look at the jury but straight away I realised this would be hard. All I wanted to do was keep my eyes on the monster that had killed my daughter; give him nowhere to look and nowhere to hide. And as I reached the witness box and entered it, there he was. Amid the sea of unfamiliar faces, the judge – high up to my right – the jury, the court recorder, the row of barristers and policemen, there *he* was, in his now-familiar outfit of what looked a little like a nice clean school uniform; the monster who was the antithesis of a well-dressed and well-behaved school boy and who'd taken the life of my beautiful, precious daughter – broken her skull just as he'd broken her school pencils. Finally, there he was, sitting there flanked by his defence team and the Vinney Green guards, head down and scribbling on a pad.

Jill came to stand in front of me, holding a card for me to read. I had chosen to take my oath on the Bible and now I took it from her and, while holding it, read the oath.

That formality done, it was time to begin.

'Mrs Aylward,' said Mr Taylor, once he was ready to start his questions. 'Could you please tell the court how long you have known Joshua Davies and what impression you had of him?'

I took a deep breath, and I began.

I'm not sure if I believe in a sixth sense or not but, as I stood in that witness box, I could feel the eyes of Davies's mother on me. She was sitting with her family just behind and to the side of me, so I couldn't actually see her but I could sense her presence and I wondered what it must feel like to be her in that moment, knowing just how much (and I don't doubt she did know) I would love to have leapt from that box and killed her son with my bare hands. Perhaps no one except someone who has lost a child to the hands of a murderer can understand how intense that feeling is.

But I tried to rein myself in and focus all my concentration on Gregg Taylor QC, the prosecution barrister, who was doing his best to help me feel at ease as I answered his questions. I told him how Josh had always seemed such a nice, polite, chatty boy and how he'd almost felt like part of the family; how he'd visited us and stayed with us many times over the years and how he'd laugh and joke and lark about with me all the time. I told him how a part of me, however, had been very cross with him that past year. He'd finished with Becca back in the January so abruptly, without any warning or apparent reason, and the prospect of him being back in our lives now had worried me: would he break her heart all over again? He'd certainly been less than kind to her over the ensuing months, as, over time, had a number of his friends.

I told him how Josh had started trying to be nice to Becca again recently, however, and how excited she'd been at that development; how, despite feeling so angry with Josh for messing Becca about, I swallowed my irritation for her sake. It was what she wanted, so I decided I was prepared to give him a second chance and agreed to him coming over to stay.

I told Mr Taylor about that morning; about the bath I'd run for Becca, about the breakfast I'd made for her, Jack and Jessica, about how it had been like any other Saturday morning, really, with all the kids squabbling over the TV remote control and making their different plans for the day.

I told him of the discussions about which of the two new hoodies Becca should wear for her date with Josh and how, as the morning went on, she tried to persuade Jess and Jack to go with her and how I hadn't appreciated the significance of this, and how difficult it had been for us to come to terms with as a family – particularly Jack, who had idolised Josh and looked up to him like a big brother.

I broke down then, which, perhaps, was inevitable. It came out of nowhere – this big uncontrollable whoosh of emotion as the image of how Jack had looked when I'd told him came to me; an image of such distress – of such complete shock and devastation – as he tried to take in how the boy he'd so idolised could have done such a thing to his sister.

'A glass of water and some tissues for Mrs Aylward, please,' said the judge immediately. Then in a softer tone, 'Would you like to take a break, Mrs Aylward?'

I shook my head and accepted the glass and box of tissues that were swiftly handed to me. 'No,' I said, wiping the tears away, 'I'd like to carry on.'

I looked at Davies as I did so, willing him to feel an iota of emotion. And for a moment – a fleeting instant – I saw something cross his face. Had that hit him? Thinking of Jack and how he'd been so much his hero; that what he'd done had destroyed something so important to my little boy? Did it hit him that he'd ruined everything – that he'd never be a hero to anyone ever again?

I didn't know but the moment passed almost as it happened. He looked down again and went back to the endless, endless doodling, as if he'd mentally shut his ears or, perhaps, that he didn't actually care. 'To show emotion,' I remember him telling Jack once, 'is to show weakness.' And perhaps it was easy for him not to show any emotion because, where there is emotion, there is humanity and, as I was coming to realise, the further I looked into the background behind the cold-blooded murder he'd committed, humanity was something he didn't possess.

Once we'd establish the events before Becca had left the house, Mr Taylor brought out a large map of the Aberkenfig and Sarn area and asked me to confirm, based on our phone conversations and the CCTV footage the police had, if the route marked in red was the one Becca had taken. Seeing it set out on a map was a shock for me and I stared at it for some seconds, realising just how convoluted a journey she'd made. At Davies's direction, she'd had Linda drop her off at Sarn Station in the end – a fact that Linda had apparently told me at the time but which, in my panic, I'd not fully taken in. Why Sarn? It made no sense at all.

It took me back to those texts and phone calls and my increasing incredulity that he'd had her walk such a bizarre route to meet him. I recalled how I'd asked Becca why, if he'd been at home like he'd told her, he'd had her walk all the way up to Church Street to meet him when doing so meant she walked past the end of his own street. And now, seeing it laid bare, it was all so obvious: he had never been where he'd said he was. He'd never been where he told his parents he was either. At the time he was talking to her – leading her in directions that meant she'd be in the area where Josh Humphreys lived – he'd been somewhere else altogether: in Café 107, plotting my daughter's death while eating breakfast.

Mr Taylor then handed me an exhibit. It was the bottle of nail varnish I'd finally found for them months into the investigation and, as I took it, he asked me to tell the court about it. 'Can you describe it for the jury?' he asked, 'and read what it says on the bottle?'

I did so, reading the words and confirming for the jury that it was indeed the nail varnish Becca had been wearing to meet Josh that day. I didn't yet know how much significance there would be to this detail but there clearly was some; I would have to wait and see.

We then moved on again, to the texts and phone calls that were made and received that evening, particularly the ones from Davies to me, which were actually meant for Becca, saying, 'Come home, Becca, we're all worried about you.' Mr Taylor also read out the various posts on Facebook, which were all in the same sort of vein, when all the while he'd known exactly where she was – lying lifeless in a clearing up in Pennsylvania Woods because it was he who had taken her there and killed her.

I finished answering Mr Taylor's questions and we then broke for lunch – a break I was very glad to take. It had been so harrowing, baring my soul in front of so many strangers, and, much as I'd wanted to come face to face with Davies, it had been more difficult than I'd imagined sitting just feet from him.

I needed space now, to clear my mind, ready for the defence cross-examination, which I'd been told would happen directly after lunch. I knew what to expect – that the barrister would attempt to discredit some of my evidence but, on that count, I wasn't concerned. How can you discredit truth? There was nothing he could ask that would change it.

Another thing that lifted my spirits was the knowledge that, in calling me, they really must be clutching at straws. Both the police and Witness Care had already told me that a defence team in a case such as this would normally try not to call the victim's mother, for obvious reasons – after all, they already had detailed statements. So the fact that they'd done so meant they had very little else.

I already knew that Davies had originally tried to point the finger at Josh Humphreys. He had lied to me that very evening, after he'd already killed her, telling me Becca had told him she'd go and 'kill some time with Josh Humphreys' while waiting for Josh to return from his grandmother's house – a place he didn't go to until after he had murdered her. But that had obviously soon become untenable, so he'd changed tack. The defence was now pointing the finger in a different direction; according to Davies, it was Ninnis who'd apparently killed Becca, not him, and the questions put to me by the defence barrister, Mr Peter Rouch QC, were obviously geared towards this version of events.

There was much questioning about what I knew of Ninnis as a person, which I couldn't really answer as I hardly knew him at all. I'd only known *of* him and much of what I knew had been via Davies who, though apparently his best friend, also seemed happy to talk about him, telling me that Ninnis was 'jealous because he fancies Becca but he can't have her because she's mine'. Mr Rouch seemed determined, however, to get me to say that I didn't like him. But how could I say that? I didn't even know him.

Not that I hadn't formed an opinion.

Mr Rouch didn't ask me about that, however. He seemed more anxious to know if Becca could swim. 'No,' I said because she had never been able to swim.

'But let's just say she could swim a little,' he persisted, bouncing on his feet in what seemed an excitable manner.

'*No*,' I repeated firmly. 'She could not swim AT ALL. She was nervous of water,' I added, wondering quite why he was so keen to get me to say that she *could* swim. 'She wouldn't even paddle in the sea.'

Again, it would be a while before I found out the significance of his apparent determination to have me answer otherwise and also an early indication of his body language, which I soon learned to read like a book. In the meantime, it seemed he was done with me.

'No more questions, m'lord,' he said, returning to his seat.

It was such a relief to have completed my evidence. Now I could finally sit in court myself and listen. And next up was

Linda, who'd been so strong and such an incredible support to me, and who now had to go through the same ordeal as I had, having been my rock since the day Becca was taken from me.

Taken from all *of us*, I remember thinking as I sat and listened to my sister having to relive the same horrors as I had that morning. And seeing her in the witness stand, I really wanted it to be over for her as soon as possible, even though I knew, like me, she was determined to be heard. She was such a strong person, so much like a mum to me, but I could tell she was in such pain and I wanted her to be done with it so I could be with her and support her too.

We'd been told by Mr Taylor to try and just give yes or no answers but, like me, Linda wanted to say more. Just as I had earlier, she spoke of how much we'd all been so fond of Josh; how, as I didn't drive, she, too, had got to know him over the years, often picking him up and dropping him off home again for Becca. She talked of how the mood had changed during that trip to drop Becca off to meet him from excitement to increasing irritation that he kept messing her about, changing the time and the meeting place. And at one point, peculiarly, saying something that prompted Becca to reply, 'Oh, it's OK, we have a new car.' We would never know what he'd said to prompt that as, unlike his texts, the police couldn't retrieve it, but what had that meant? Had he been hiding somewhere, stalking Linda's car?

Like me, when she was done, Linda was hugely relieved that it was over, though for her, she said, the most difficult thing had been looking into the eyes of Davies as she gave her evidence. She'd wanted to meet his eyes, just as I had, but she had found it chilling. 'It was horrible,' she told me. 'I've never seen him look at me like that before. He just stared and stared at me out of those dark, soulless eyes. So much hate, as if he wanted to kill me.'

Again, far from answers, all the day had seemed to throw up were more questions. But as Linda joined the family and me in the public gallery, I knew all that was about to change. The next witness to be questioned was to be Liam Thomas. Now, for the first time since the nightmare began, I was going to find out what had happened to my daughter.

CHAPTER SEVENTEEN

TAKING THE STAND

Thursday, 23 June 2011

The evidence due to be given by Liam Thomas and Daniel Ninnis would be presented to the court in two parts. First, we would be shown video evidence of the statements both boys had made to the police at Cardiff Bay custody suite. We would then see them take the stand and give their evidence to the court, although, because they were minors, they would not appear in the courtroom itself; they would be interviewed in an adjacent room and their testimony would be streamed live via video link to a screen that was erected in the court.

I braced myself for the moment when the screen would flicker into life. Now, at last, I was going to hear the full story...

It was at around 11am, according to Liam Thomas, when he was dropped off at Café 107 by his mother to meet Josh Davies and Daniel Ninnis for breakfast. The café was in the main street in Aberkenfig and was a regular haunt of theirs; they would meet there most Saturdays for breakfast. Liam was on crutches at the time – a point that would become key later on – after a recent injury he'd sustained playing rugby. After about three quarters of an hour they walked up to Daniel Ninnis's house on Dunraven Street, where Daniel's parents were packing to go on a camping trip. At this point, Josh was busy typing and sending a text to someone and, when Liam asked him who it was, Josh told him it was Becca. It was well-known at that time that Josh had made comments to various people in school that he'd like to kill her, not least to Liam himself, who assumed he must have been joking.

Daniel's parents left, leaving the three boys alone in the house, and it was shortly after this that Josh told the boys of his plan to meet with Becca in the forest, with the intention of killing her. They discussed possible ways of doing it for some time, Daniel even going out to the garden shed to get shovels so that they could act out various methods of killing her. Josh then told the boys to bring the shovels up to the forest later, so they could use them to help bury her body.

At this point, Liam Thomas testified that he didn't actually believe Joshua would go through with it, even when, upon leaving Daniel's house at around 1pm, his parting words were apparently that 'the time has come' and, once again, telling them that his intention was to kill Becca.

He was gone for about an hour and a half. At this point, Liam decided to get in touch with Josh to find out what was happening, sending a text to ask where he was and whether he was OK. Getting no reply, he then decided to ring Josh instead, who now answered and told him to go down and meet him at the end of the street. Liam and Daniel did so but, after 10 minutes and having sent another text saying, 'come on', they gave up and walked back to Daniel's.

Once indoors, they went back to watching television for a few minutes while waiting to hear from Josh before finally calling him again – this time getting a response – and asking why he had failed to show up as promised. Josh replied that the reason was because he was still up in the forest and, when Liam asked if he was with Becca, he apparently giggled and then gave the answer, 'Define with?' He then asked both the boys to go and meet him at the forest entrance, which they did, getting there at around 2.40pm.

They waited at the entrance to the forest for some time, ringing Josh several times without success. Finally, however, Josh texted, asking Daniel to ring him, although, since it was Liam who had the phone (Daniel's phone was apparently broken), it was Liam who called him. Josh immediately asked to speak to Daniel. Daniel duly took the phone and, after listening for a while, said, 'OK, I'll be there now,' then came off the phone, saying Josh sounded panicky and that he was going up to meet him at the top of the forest.

Liam was unable to go with him. The hill was steep and slippery and, being on crutches, he knew he'd struggle to get to the top so, instead, he waited at the entrance while Daniel ran up. Liam's wait was short – it was only a matter of minutes before both boys returned, Daniel telling him that he'd seen Becca for himself, just lying there, face down on the earth. Josh, who Liam noticed didn't seem particularly fazed by that, suggested they go back to Daniel's.

Once back indoors, Josh described what he'd done. He told them that he had, indeed, killed her. He said that while Becca had been facing the other way, he'd gone up behind her and hit her with a rock. She'd fallen down then, he told them, and wouldn't stop screaming, so he hit her again repeatedly till she did.

Liam then testified that he'd asked Josh if there had been any blood, to which he'd replied that yes, there had been some, on the rock, which he said he'd thrown away into a bush. He also mentioned that there had been blood on Becca's face as well, which was why he'd turned her over onto her front. That way, he said, nobody could see it.

Joshua then went into the kitchen and made them all a cup of tea. In his absence, both the other boys expressed disbelief at what had happened, as well as at Josh's apparent lack of emotion about what he'd done. Liam, who had by now decided that things 'didn't feel right', texted his mother and asked her to come and pick him up. She arrived at 4pm and he left with her but, before he did so, Josh told him to delete all his texts – as he himself would – and that, if anyone asked, to tell them they had been together all afternoon.

Liam Thomas's evidence was incredibly difficult to watch. To see him sitting there in a room that looked similar to the one in Coity, where Jess had given her video evidence the previous winter, and describing the murder of my daughter so clinically was so distressing to watch that I had to put my hands over my ears. In the end, Linda and I even had to walk out of court for a bit, unable to bear it. I felt physically sick. It sounded and looked so cold and callous, so lacking in any sort of feeling. He could have been describing the plot of a horror film to his friends.

DC Carol Saunders, bless her, came out to check that we were both OK.

'Remember,' she said gently, 'that all he is doing is repeating what Davies has told him. And Davies is a liar.' That was such a sweet thing for her to do.

It couldn't help but get to us, though. How could it fail to get to any decent human being? Here was this boy – no, more accurately, this young *man* – and he had heard all this and done nothing about it. Peter Rouch QC might have had a different motivation for asking the question (he was set on proving Ninnis was the killer, of course), but I wanted the same question as him answered.

'How,' he wanted to know, reading out various Facebook and text messages Thomas had posted, 'how could you be talking about having a lovely meal and watching TV when there is a young girl lying dead in the forest?'

Thomas apparently didn't have an answer.

'And leaving Daniel Ninnis's house,' he went on, referring to when Liam Thomas was collected by his mother, 'you actually drove past a police station. Did it not once occur to you to call the police? Phone for an ambulance?'

No, it seemed. It didn't.

Daniel Ninnis gave evidence next and his story was similar and equally gruesome to have to listen to. He also talked of Liam and Josh having already struck a deal about breakfast in a text exchange that would soon become headline news all over Britain:

Josh: What would you do if I actually did kill her?

Liam: Oh, I'd buy you breakfast, mate.

And there was more. On the Thursday there was another flurry of texts:

Josh: Don't say anything but you may just owe me breakfast.

Liam: Best text I have ever had, mate. Seriously, if it is true, I am happy to pay for a breakfast.

Josh: I hope by then it will be done and dusted.

Liam: I want all the details. You sadistic bastard. :)

Josh: Large breakfast with extras of everything.

Liam: Sick, sick boy.

Ninnis also spoke of Josh after taking a call from Becca – who at this point was getting ready to go and meet her – saying things to Liam like, 'today's the day' and 'well, the time has come today'. He said he'd asked both boys what it was they were talking and joking about, and that Joshua's reply was, 'Oh, I'm going to meet her and I'm going to kill her.'

Ninnis also reported that, although once back at his house Josh repeated this threat, neither he nor Liam Thomas actually believed he would go through with it. He said that when they were playing with the spade and shovel from the shed, they were all laughing and joking; they weren't taking Josh seriously at all.

Ninnis's account of what had happened closely tallied with Thomas's but I knew that it would differ in one important respect. I would now have to sit and listen to what happened when he left Liam by the roadside and went up to join Davies in the forest itself. At the point of meeting Davies, Ninnis was still using Thomas's phone. He recounted that, as he reached the top, where the land fell away on either side to a pair of gorges, he could both hear Josh on the phone and in person. He then saw him and walked across to him, puffed out from the steep climb to get up there, and Josh told him where the body was, pointing towards Becca as he spoke, commenting, 'There's no blood on me, luckily.' He then suggested that Ninnis lift the hood and take a look at Becca's face but he had declined. Both boys, slightly panicked now, according to Ninnis, then ran back down to where Thomas was still waiting at the entrance to the forest and where Liam immediately asked if Becca was dead.

They then walked back to Daniel's house, where Josh told them what he'd done. 'I tried to break her neck,' he said, 'but that didn't work very well, so I used a rock. I started hitting her with it but she wouldn't stop screaming.'

Joshua then made tea for them all and called his grandmother, asking her to pick him up and take him back to her house. Like Thomas, Daniel Ninnis reported being in a state of disbelief.

After Thomas and Davies left, Daniel was once again alone in the house and, deciding he didn't want to stay there overnight on his own, he tried to contact his mother but her phone was switched off. He then telephoned Joshua, who asked his grandfather to drive down and pick Daniel up and take him to be with Joshua at his grandmother's. At some point during the evening, he noted in his statement, he recalled Davies taking a call from me and hearing him tell me he hadn't seen Becca at all that day.

Most interesting to me, watching Ninnis's original testimony from the Cardiff Bay custody suite being played, was the effect it seemed to be having on Davies, who was obviously also sat listening to it in court. It was the first time I'd seen him really engage with what was happening around him. He looked anxious and stressed and very uncomfortable in his skin, as perhaps he would be, when I thought about it. After all, his grounds for pleading not guilty to murder were that he maintained that Ninnis, his supposed (and presumably now, former) best friend, had been the one who had actually committed the crime.

Perhaps the knowledge that Ninnis himself would soon be cross-examined via video link – as Liam Thomas had before him – was beginning to prove too much for Davies. In any event, during the final break, after which Ninnis's evidence would continue, his defence lawyer asked the judge if we could finish early for the day as the defendant was feeling unwell with a sore throat.

But the judge wasn't happy: he argued that a doctor could attend the court then and there and examine him, upon which the defence suggested Davies could perhaps be seen by the doctor at Vinney Green on his return instead.

'No,' the judge said firmly, 'that will not be tolerated, I'm afraid. He must be back in court at ten o'clock tomorrow morning.'

Friday, 24 June 2011

Yet again I spent the night plagued by horrible images. I was also confused now, not knowing the exact course of events; not knowing exactly what Davies had done to Becca or what part, if any, Ninnis might have played in it, even though I didn't doubt Davies had been the killer because the evidence was overwhelming.

I was dreading the next day, when I knew I'd have to listen to even more of it, when both Mr Taylor and Mr Rouch cross-examined Ninnis. But even then, would I ever know exactly what Davies did to Becca?

I tried to put it out of my mind; to focus on Jack and Jessica and what they needed, to keep my mask in place. All the while, bit by bit, I felt like I was dying inside.

And it seemed I wasn't the only one who had no choice but to grit my teeth and get on with it. Davies and his team were also in place the following morning, just as the judge had directed, presumably having been passed fit enough to attend.

The day was due to start with the resumption of Daniel Ninnis's cross-examination but the defence team had other matters to attend to first. Apparently, Ninnis had been on Skype the night before telling friends about what had happened during court the previous day, including asking, 'Guess who pulled a sickie because I was giving evidence?' So as opposed to watching more of Ninnis's pre-recorded evidence, they had him live on screen from his video link in the adjacent room in the courthouse where, instead of being asked about the murder, he was first reprimanded by the judge and warned – as everyone was in court, every day – that the case must not be discussed outside of court.

I thought he was an idiot. What had he been thinking? That bit of crowing had potentially cataclysmic implications, as it might have jeopardised the whole trial. Was he trying to pull some kind of double bluff? Create a mistrial and get his friend off? Somehow, since Davies was attempting to get him tried for murder, I doubted it. And I was relieved when we were able to resume with proceedings. I'd been right the first time, I decided – he was just an idiot.

That small drama over, the jury were then brought in and another day began, this one being the one where Ninnis was cross-examined by both prosecution and defence.

The next few days saw a succession of expert witnesses take the stand. Here was the fruition of all those months and months of police work and, at long last, answers to my endless, endless questions about the significance of so many seemingly unrelated things – as well as things I'd known nothing about at all.

There was also a brief breathing space: the jury had asked to be taken to the scene of the crime and also to walk the same route as Becca had taken that Saturday, to get a clearer picture of the sequence of events. This left us with a free day and a chance to spend time as a family with the children, though we were fearful of going out because the trial was so high-profile and we knew the press would be onto us like a shot. I didn't want that; nor did I want to see, hear or read anything in the media or on TV, although I'd arranged for a friend to get and keep copies of all the press coverage as I knew that, at some point, I would need – if not want – to read it all.

Wednesday, 6 July 2011

We returned to court on the Wednesday. Except that now it was a different court. The original, or Old Court, as it's known, was just across the road from Court 1 and we had already been told that, at some point, should the trial go on for longer than a couple of weeks, we would have to move in there, since another big murder trial would be commencing – one which required the greater capacity of Court 1. For me, this was the best news imaginable.

We had given our evidence, obviously, but Davies still had to give his and, unlike Ninnis and Thomas, he did not have the luxury of being cross-examined from a room down the corridor. He was 16 and charged with murder; everything he had to say would be said from the witness box in court. And I couldn't have been more pleased. Because, unlike the largely unthreatening Court 1, with all its modern styling, the Old Court, though smaller, was much more imposing. Intimidating, high-ceilinged and old-fashioned, it was a court that looked just like the average person would imagine – a sombre and scary enough place to be for anyone, but particularly the defendant in a murder trial, even if it could never be quite as horrific as the place where my child had spent her last moments on earth. But my pleasure at this news was tempered by anxiety. As soon as I knew the order of events, I also knew this would be a day in which my brother Roger's caution would apply; today I would definitely need to brace myself.

Proceedings began with two further witnesses, both friends, or perhaps more accurately, *former* friends of Davies: Dan Carter and Jean Luc Howe. Both confirmed what by now seemed common knowledge at Archbishop McGrath High School – that Davies had talked to them more than once about his intention to kill Becca.

They then moved on to the murder weapon itself. At this point, I was aware of what had happened. I had the basic fact of there being such a thing imprinted on my brain; I knew Becca had been struck and I also knew whatever had struck her had killed her. I had sat through the statements and cross-examination of both Liam Thomas and Daniel Ninnis too. But to have to actually *see* that thing – that rock – mere feet from me in court was something I expected to find deeply traumatic.

And it was. Exhibit AN1 was brought into proceedings by Detective Sergeant Ed Griffiths, the Scenes of Crime officer: a big man, he was well over 6ft in height, not fat and not massively muscular, but very burly. He confirmed that it had been found five metres away from Becca at 3.45pm on Monday, 25 October 2010. It had been located after two specialist dogs had found it on separate searches.

I was prepared for what I was about to see because Mr Taylor had already mentioned it, before DS Griffiths took it from a large plastic box that had been brought into court and, after showing it close up to every member of the jury, placed it on the bench directly in front of the judge.

I had felt nauseous for much of the time since my daughter had been taken from me – sick with fear, sick with anxiety, sick with nerves, sick with disgust – but seeing that rock sickened me in a way that was different again. It was so big and heavy that the Detective Sergeant had some difficulty holding it – even in both of his big, strong hands.

I felt sickened to think that such a huge, ugly lump of solid rock had been the last thing to touch my beautiful girl. My anger raged inside, so much so that it was a good thing that we were in Swansea Criminal Crown Court now, rather than in the law courts because, had we been there, Davies would have been a mere couple of feet from me – killing distance. And I had no doubt that I would have taken full advantage of the opportunity.

To think that this monster – this monster who had often bragged, actually *bragged*, about his father being so strong that he'd managed to break another man's skull with his bare hands (although whether this is true or not, I have no idea) – had taken this rock and used it to break the skull of a girl who was so tiny and so frail. How could any living, breathing human *not* feel sick at such a barbaric act?

Thursday, 7 July 2011

Previously I had known nothing about the rather gruesomely named 'cadaver dogs' the police used in cases such as these but I was about to be educated, as were the jury. The first officer to take the stand that day explained that these were dogs who were trained to sniff out human traces and, once they had found what they were looking for, would 'freeze' in front of the item concerned.

The dogs in this case were three mature English Springer Spaniels called Muzzy and Badge, who were both operated by their dog handler, PC Brake, and Tito, who was operated by PC Richards. They were taken to the crime scene on Monday, 25 October 2010 – the first day of intensive forensic examination – and operated one dog at a time.

Muzzy and Badge were first; one by one they were taken around the murder scene for 10–15 minutes at a time and both dogs did the 'freeze' indication at one particular rock. They were then taken some distance away and left to search again without their operators. Again, both dogs managed to locate the rock.

The same process happened with Tito once PC Richards had arrived and, with Tito also identifying the same rock as the other dogs, it was duly bagged and recorded. It was also noted that there was no vegetation beneath it, indicating that it had not been where it was found for very long.

Now we were getting into the territory of the crime scene and the forensic evidence that was being admitted. The jury had been given a portfolio of information: images of the scene itself, various facts and figures about logistics and timings, and, of course, images of Becca's body where she lay. And because we were now sitting in the public gallery just above the court, looking down, I could see the photographs the members of the jury held in their hands. With each flip of the page they were directed to look at, I could see the photos were being progressively zoomed in and, at one point, I could clearly see Becca's red hoodie, a splash of cheerful scarlet amid a dark background of fallen leaves. At this point I chose to look away.

The day continued with the admission of more forensic evidence. All those months I'd been waiting on the results of the police endeavours and here they were, laid out before me. It was an impressive haul. I had always known that the police had worked tirelessly but was overwhelmed, nevertheless, by the sheer painstaking detail involved. Within the first 48 hours, so many processes had taken place and so many experts had played their crucial part. There had been a soil expert to analyse the ground on which she lay, a consultant pathologist, whose job it was to take Becca's body to hospital, the cadaver dogs, of course, together with their painstaking handlers, a Scenes of Crime officer, plus various photographers and forensic pathologists.

All took the stand; all took their oath. All recounted the part they had played in the investigation. All took the time to explain to the jury the significance of the things they'd found and analysed.

And as I sat and watched them I felt Becca's presence keenly. This was the world she'd so wanted to be a part of: a world where hardworking, diligent professionals came together to carry out their responsibilities to ensure justice was done. And I felt a small comfort in knowing that, however grim those responsibilities were for the people undertaking them (and how could anyone fail to be upset, having to document the minutiae of such horror?), all had played their part in getting justice for my daughter. I was immensely grateful to them all.

There was, of course, another scene that required forensic examination and, as the day progressed, the focus moved to the immediate aftermath and the arresting officer, DC Tristan Evans, took the stand.

DC Evans recounted that, together with four other detective constables, he had arrived at the address of Davies's grandmother's at 9.50am on the Sunday. Having been invited in, DCs Evans and Rees then went upstairs to a bedroom, where they found three teenage boys asleep. Davies was in the bed on the right, Ninnis in the one to the left and Davies's cousin Tyler was on the floor between them.

DC Evans first spoke to Davies, telling him that he was arresting him on suspicion of the murder of Rebecca Aylward, to which Davies, 'groggy from waking up, not intoxicated, unfazed, no reaction', answered, 'I was with Daniel and Liam yesterday.'

DC Rees then took the stand and corroborated DC Evans' evidence, recounting that he told Ninnis that he was investigating the death of Rebecca Aylward and that he, too, was under arrest.

Both boys were then handcuffed at the front and taken out to waiting police cars, which would take them separately to custody suites in Cardiff Bay. As they left, Davies told his grandmother, 'They think I've killed Rebecca.' What his grandmother said in response wasn't recorded. Ninnis, however, was recorded as asking, 'Why am I being arrested? Rebecca is Josh's friend.'

Over the next 48 hours more vital evidence was recovered. That same evening another crime investigator, CI Tarstan Patel, went to Davies's grandmother's house and recovered a black hoodie that was hanging over a sofa in the lounge. He also found and recovered a purple T-shirt and a pair of Converse-style trainers from the washing machine; they were wet.

It was then the turn of Mr Justin Scott, a forensic scientist from London, who was an expert on fibres, blood and DNA profiles, to take the stand. He explained the various processes he used for recovering evidence and said that he had recovered some 300 fibres from the rock that had been used to kill Becca. These had included red tufts from her jacket, black viscose tufts from inside the hood and several from the hoodie that CI Patel had recovered from Davies's grandmother's house.

Questioned by Mr Taylor, Mr Scott reported two important facts: that, although both were dark fibres, there was no chance Becca's jacket-hood fibres could be mistaken for those of Davies's hoodie and that the 12 fibres from the latter found on the stone did not get there by accident.

'Did the fibres from TP4 [Davies's jacket] have direct contact with the stone?' Mr Taylor asked him.

'Yes,' he said. 'I would not expect to find 12 by chance.'

Another forensic scientist took the stand then. It had been Dr Sarah Jacob's task to analyse ink fragments that had been found at the scene and, finally, the importance of the bottle of nail varnish became clear. The bottle of polish I had described to the jury when I'd taken that stand just a few days ago could now be positively matched, both to the fragments found in the bags in which they'd encased Becca's hands and to the rock with which Davies had killed her.

But it was a small detail, about something found at Davies's grandmother's house several days later, which would, on the following day, give me the biggest shock yet.

CHAPTER EIGHTEEN

DAVIES'S STORY

Friday, 8 July 2011

By now I knew a great deal about the events of the previous October 23rd, as well as quite a lot about the threats that had preceded it. But I did not yet understand the significance of the testimony of PC Townsend, who'd visited Davies's grandmother's house on 28 October. He had conducted a search and had taken away a number of items, including a white plastic pot that had been found in the back garden shed. A Halloween pot, of the kind used by children to go trick or treating, it had been found on the floor of the shed to the left of a PlayStation and some gardening books, slightly hidden from view.

For me this piece of evidence was key. And not just because it was part of the search of those premises, it was key because of what it suggested to *me*.

The pot and its contents – a murky brown liquid containing

a number of seeds – had been taken away and sent for analysis to Ian Humphreys, another forensic scientist, who specialised in poisons, drugs and bodily fluids. Having established that the contents included nicotine, caffeine and 21 seeds, he sent the contents to another scientist, Professor Monique Simmonds, of the Royal Botanic Gardens, Kew, who was an expert in the chemistry of plants.

As Professor Simmonds recounted what she'd found after her various tests, I watched with a growing and terrible realisation that a horrific truth might be emerging. Simmonds talked about the contents of the container and how each component was analysed separately, and of various compounds that she'd established were present. She talked of finding liquid digoxin, of digitonin, of the plant concerned being the foxglove, and of finding two cardiac glycosides present also.

It was a lot to take in – I'm not a scientist and so much of it made no sense to me but the words that leapt out were familiar from childhood; that she was talking about foxgloves – digitalis was obtained from them – and what I'd had drummed into me, like any other child, was that foxgloves were highly poisonous.

Transfixed, I watched as Mr Taylor asked for her conclusion about the pot and contents. The liquid had contained foxgloves, she told him, the leaves of which were poisonous, and the traditional way of creating a poison from foxgloves was to crush them using a pestle and mortar. I was obviously yet to find out the connection between this pot and its contents and Davies, but already one thing seemed startlingly clear: he had apparently been trying to make poison.

To poison Becca? Was that the reason for all the illness she'd suffered? I could hardly believe what I was hearing but was this behind all those months of nausea and blackouts? Had all those brain scans been for nothing? Was *this* why she'd been so ill? Friday, 8 July wasn't just the day of this staggering revelation, however, it was also the day when, after over two weeks of testimony and evidence, Davies himself was to finally take centre stage, instead of sitting there doodling on his notepad.

It had been a long journey already and I had learned a great deal. Much of it had been confirmation of what I already knew – that Davies had murdered my daughter – but some of it had been shocking and revelatory. What had really begun to sink in now was the scale of it. From what I'd already seen and heard, I had known this was never an impulsive crime of passion: it had been planned in great detail, over a period of many months, by someone who appeared not to have a shred of human emotion, bar a desire to commit murder.

For the defence team, however, this simply wasn't true. The defence team maintained that the 'truth' Davies still insisted upon was the real one; that it had not been him but his best friend of over a decade, Daniel Ninnis, who was Becca's murderer.

It was at this point that I agreed to let Jess come to court with me. She'd begged and begged, and I'd refused, feeling the evidence and various exhibits would all be too harrowing, but now I accepted that she had the right to watch her sister's killer take the stand. But before he could do so, however, his interview discs needed to be shown, beginning with his first: recorded at Cardiff Bay custody suite on 25 October 2010, at 10.50am. However, unlike for Ninnis and Thomas, there were no soft furnishings or reassuring officers to put the young witness at his ease; he was in a stark interview room, having been charged with Becca's murder.

In his interview, Davies confirmed that he'd gone to Café 107 in Aberkenfig on the day of the murder, just as Ninnis and Thomas before him. He had arranged with Becca that he was to meet her and go back to stay at her house later and exchanged texts with her while in the café with his friends.

After one such text, according to his version of events, he turned to Liam and said, 'Looks like you're going to be buying me breakfast,' at which Liam started to laugh, causing Davies to repeat himself, pointedly adding, 'You'll see.' This was a joke, he maintained – a joke the boys had recently shared between them about how Joshua was going to kill Rebecca.

Once at Daniel's house after breakfast and with Daniel's parents by now having left to go camping, he received a call on his mobile from Becca. They discussed where to meet, settled on Pandy Park and, apparently, spoke about some sort of plan to 'freak Liam out'.

By 2pm, still at Daniel's, having not yet gone to meet Becca, he maintained that he took another call from her (in reality, at 1pm), which he went into the conservatory to take. During this call, they apparently arranged to meet on Church Street, close to where Daniel lived, and a short time later, she sent a text to say she'd arrived there. As he left, there was another short joking exchange, with Liam saying, 'The time has come,' (a thing he often said, apparently) and, as Joshua left the house, 'Good luck.'

Joshua then walked to meet Becca, who was apparently under a tree sheltering from the rain and at that point on the phone to her mother. They stayed under the tree for 15 minutes or so, trying to keep dry and chatting, including Joshua telling Becca about the bet he'd had with Liam about killing her and Liam saying if he did, he'd buy him breakfast. They apparently spoke about how they could make Liam think they'd done it, with Becca apparently commenting 'he'd find out' he hadn't when she 'walked into school on Monday'.

Joshua apparently agreed, saying it would be funny to see the look on his face, as he'd been so certain that he 'couldn't get rid of you'. He suggested a plan then, the idea being that they'd go somewhere and have Becca lie on the ground so that Liam thought she was dead but she apparently refused because the ground would be wet. In the end, they'd apparently hit on a compromise: that they would go up to Pennsylvania Woods. If they did it there, Liam (being on crutches) wouldn't actually be able to get up there to see the 'body'. Josh could, therefore, tell him he'd done the deed but he wouldn't actually be able to check.

They then walked from Church Street to the main street and on the way Becca's phone went. It was her Auntie Linda, asking if she wanted picking up and taking home, but Becca said no. They continued to walk up to the wood's entrance and then up a well-trodden path, finally turning right, close to the edge of one of the quarries. There they stopped and again discussed the plan to fool Liam but, again, Becca decided that the ground was too wet so they once more set off to find another, better spot. Once there, Joshua texted Liam asking him to call him and, when he did, asking whether the deed had been done yet, Joshua had told him yes, and to come up and take a look.

He then took two further calls from Daniel Ninnis, wanting directions to where he was. There was then a third, saying Ninnis was now on his way. Joshua and Becca were now laughing about their plan and, when Daniel arrived, he was clearly unhappy at having been duped. He apparently laughed himself, sarcastically – something he did when annoyed – and, according to Davies, must have mistook Becca saying something to Josh about going back to her house for the pair of them having a laugh at his expense.

In any event, the next thing Josh knew was that Daniel had grabbed Becca by the wrist and had pulled her before pushing her on the shoulder so she fell onto the ground. Face down on the floor, she apparently told Daniel to 'fuck off', upon which he picked up a rock (just slightly smaller than a sheet of A4 paper) and struck her on the back of the head with it. She screamed then but remained where she was on the ground, while Daniel hit her six or seven times with the rock, at one point, Joshua noted, causing a loud cracking noise that he thought might be her skull.

Joshua believed, he told the officers, that Becca was now dead and admitted that he'd done nothing while Daniel was hitting her because, though he tried to say stop, he was in shock.

Liam Thomas called out then, wanting to know where they were. Upon which Daniel called out, 'You should see the body!' Daniel then ran off and a second later Joshua ran after him, noticing as they ran that, at some point, Daniel threw the rock forwards in the direction of the quarry. The three boys then returned to Daniel's house.

I was struck by so many inconsistencies in Davies's version of events that I was already furiously ticking them off in my brain by the time the video evidence of his second interview under caution was ready to play.

What had he said Becca had said? 'He'll find out when I walk into school on Monday'? I knew Becca would never have said something like that because they had just broken up for half term – it was the sort of detail she wouldn't have forgotten. If there was one thing she'd never do, it would be to say she'd be walking into school that Monday; she knew she wouldn't be, she had already made plans.

Then there was the alleged phone call at 2pm; this didn't exist. I had long known that the last call Becca made had been to me: she'd been on the phone to me when he'd finally come into view at 1.19pm. The phone wasn't used again after that. There was also the weather: it was no longer raining by 2pm, it had stopped just after I'd last spoken to her. I couldn't wait for Mr Taylor to cross-examine him.

During Davies's second interview while in police custody, on Monday, 25 October 2010, they also began picking holes in his version of the 'facts'. By now they had retrieved various Facebook postings and conversations that he had previously not mentioned.

'I just wanted it to go back to normal again,' he had posted. What did he mean by that? And 'I'm a chip off the old block'. (Which I inferred to mean like his father – the father who'd apparently cracked a man's skull with one blow.) The police wanted to know too, what did that mean precisely? He mumbled something about chopping wood in the garden.

They also wanted to know why he didn't he tell his gran about what Daniel had apparently done, or call the police, or ring for an ambulance, or cry for help. His reply: 'I didn't think of doing that.'

What about the text messages he'd sent to Becca's phone on the

Saturday evening then, knowing full well she was lying dead in the woods? His response to this was that he'd been 'too scared to say' and that, if I'd perhaps kept ringing him, the guilt might eventually kick in and he 'would say' – which, of course, he did not.

Davies had many answers to the police questions, almost all of them questionable. He told them that Ninnis, the supposed perpetrator, was keen for him not to be involved as he – very nobly – 'didn't want me in prison as well'.

The tapes of Davies's interviews continued until 12 July 2011, as the police, who had clearly interviewed many witnesses over an incredibly short time, asked question after question about what had gone before. They confirmed what the court by now already knew; that they had managed to find numerous people who all seemed to have reported the same thing – that Davies had, indeed, been talking about killing Becca for several months, to many people, even discussing various ways he might achieve it, which according to Davies included hatching a plan with Daniel Ninnis to drown her by throwing her off the bridge at Aberkenfig and into the quarry, even suggesting that Ninnis could perhaps make an 'attempt' to rescue her, for effect, by which time, being unable to swim, she'd have drowned.

I was stunned to hear this, but it at least made sense of why the Defence Barrister had tried so hard to get me to say Becca *could* swim at the start of the trial, as it would then discredit Ninnis's evidence against Davies; who knew very well that she couldn't.

And there was more. There was also the possibility of 'poisoning her Ribena', which, sickeningly, I already knew he'd potentially followed through with in his gran's summerhouse and which I had already heard he'd suggested to Ninnis and/or Thomas during a science lesson. Another witness, Dan Carter, said Davies had even told his own father.

'Last time you were drunk,' the interviewing police officer asked Davies, 'did you talk to your dad about killing Becca? Dan [Carter] said you told your dad. You, Ninnis and Tyler – you said you wanted to poison Becca and asked if he [Tyler] wanted to be involved.'

'No, I don't talk to Tyler much,' Davies lied.

I knew this was a lie because Tyler lived with his grandmother and Davies often stayed there at weekends.

The police officer persisted: 'You look as if you're thinking about something else,' he said. 'Have you ever said you wanted to poison Becca?'

'No, not poison,' Davies replied.

'So, tell me about the pestle and mortar,' the policeman countered.

Upon which Davies told him that a few weeks earlier, having nothing to do, he was discussing possible activities with Ninnis. They were in Davies's grandmother's kitchen and Ninnis was asking about the pestle and mortar on the worktop, wondering what it was for.

'I said it's to crush things and stuff,' he apparently told Ninnis, before asking him, 'Do you want a go?'

So they apparently went out to look 'for berries and stuff to go in it' and 'picked berries off trees and dead plants'. They then crushed them with the pestle and mortar and tipped what they'd produced into a container, then added Coke. 'Well, Ninnis did,' he finished, 'and we left it in the summerhouse.'

'What conversation were you having?' the policeman wanted to know. 'Did you discuss that it was poison?'

To which Davies replied 'yeah.'

It was almost impossible to absorb what we were hearing – how could anyone take such an appalling thing in? For what had now been proven – both forensically and via the testimony of several witnesses – was that this was, indeed, no crime of passion. This was no spur-of-the-moment fury that had ended in tragedy; no sick culmination of some angry teenage row. From what I was hearing, my worst fears for many months had been confirmed: that this animal had spent *whole months* of his life dreaming up ways in which to kill my beloved Becca. It had been pre-meditated to an almost incomprehensible degree – and over what? That's what I wanted to know. Just what had Becca done to become the object of such evil intention?

And worst of all was that Davies had even bragged and joked about it. He hadn't even kept his murderous intent to himself. No, he'd spread the word about how much he hated her – really couldn't have made his feelings plainer and even had an ongoing joke with his close friends about actually doing it. Made bets. Made poison. Even announced that 'the time has come'.

And they had told no one. Done absolutely nothing.

CHAPTER NINETEEN

OBSERVING A PSYCHOPATH

Thursday, 14 July 2011

The trial was splashed across the papers daily; it was almost impossible to avoid. And with it came what would become the media 'tagline' for Davies's murder trial – that he killed Becca for the 'price of a full English breakfast'.

There had been no court session on 13 July. Davies's defence barrister was busy on a case in another court and we took advantage of the break to get right out of town to do our shopping, in order to find the comfort of a bit of anonymity. I couldn't bear to see people who knew me because of how I knew they would react. To see the sadness on their faces, to know how they were struggling to know what to say to me, to see them wondering how to approach me, fearful that I might cry – it was all just too difficult.

I was fine when people came straight up to me and got to the point more matter of factly but displays of sympathy never failed to set me off. And I couldn't be doing that; I had to keep strong for the children. And also to keep my mind focused. It was working overtime as it was, as everything was coming together for me now – the memories flooding back. And with them and my new understanding of all that had happened, I began to finally make sense of that chaotic 24 hours. It was all beginning to slot into place, all the dates, times and details.

There was the business of a message that had been read out in court and had initially been so confusing: it had been sent sometime on the Friday, by Davies to Thomas, saying, in reference to their usual Saturday-morning breakfast gathering, that 'it will all be done and dusted by then'.

That now made sense. Davies had first planned to murder Becca on the Friday but had been thwarted by her decision to go shopping with Linda that day instead and to shunt her meeting with him back till the Saturday. Undeterred, while she dreamed excitedly about their possible reunion, he had then quickly rearranged his plans to accommodate this and so began the elaborate business of getting Becca to where he wanted her, having her meet him in a place where he felt safe from CCTV cameras and even going so far as to dress in clothes he didn't normally wear and having her tell me she'd seen Josh Humphreys when she hadn't. He'd been so calculating – these details had all been a part of his plan (along with his later lie that he'd seen them together) to get poor Josh charged with her murder.

And then, the deed done, he'd been as cold as the rock that he'd killed my daughter with. If it was designed to put the police off the scent, it was as stupid as it was arrogant; if it was bravado, it was like no kind of bravado I'd ever come across.

Whatever his motivation, what he did then will stay with me always. He had Ninnis back round to his gran's – the 'best friend' he would soon be calling Becca's murderer – and the pair of them had settled down to watch a film together: the violent murder movie, *No Country for Old Men*.

'Good day with Liam Thomas and Daniel Ninnis,' read Davies's Facebook status update at 5.24pm that Saturday. 'And a lovely breakfast. :D'

Davies was called to the witness stand at 11.10am. It was the first time since the trial had begun that he had not been seated between his guards from Vinney Green and flanked by the members of his defence counsel, and I was pleased to see just how addled he looked to see me sitting in the gallery, flanked by both Josh Humphreys, whom he'd initially tried to implicate, and another good friend of Becca's, Irving Smith. Both boys were a reassuring presence for me and, for Davies, clearly very intimidating. I was so grateful to have them there.

Davies was required to take the oath, just as everybody else did but, strikingly since he had been brought up a Catholic, he opted not to swear on the Bible. This seemed apt to me, as I knew he was not about to tell the truth.

After the formalities were over, Gregg Taylor QC launched into action, asking, 'Joshua, tell me. Did you love Rebecca?'

The huge echoing courtroom was silent. There was a long pause while Davies fidgeted and squirmed then looked towards the floor.

'What?' he mumbled eventually.

'It's a simple enough question,' Mr Taylor said. 'So, can you tell us, please – did you love Rebecca?'

It was clear to all that Davies was getting really uncomfortable, apparently finding it impossible to answer a simple yes or no question with an equally simple yes or no answer.

Mr Taylor waited. And waited. Then turned around and looked at the jury before moving on, leaving the silence to answer for him.

Just as the jury had, Davies now had a sheaf of papers to refer to, in this case dates and times and details of various key bits of evidence, including times and contents of texts and of various calls. Despite the many discrepancies between the facts and his account of what had happened, he continued to maintain that it had been Ninnis who'd killed Becca in a protracted act of rage when he had mistakenly thought Davies and Becca had been laughing at his expense.

'I was wondering if we had annoyed him a bit too much,' he added. 'I was wondering if we had gone a bit too far.'

'Did you think he might kill her?' Mr Taylor asked.

'No,' Davies answered. 'I just thought that he was angry – I didn't think that he was going to be physically violent to her.'

He then told Mr Taylor that, as per what he'd said in his original statement, Ninnis had grabbed Rebecca's wrist and pulled her towards him before pushing her onto the ground.

'You had time to step in and stop him,' Mr Taylor said. 'Why did you not act?'

'I didn't think anything was going to happen,' Davies answered.

'But here was your girlfriend,' Mr Taylor persisted, 'Five feet, two inches and six stone, on the floor, and you did nothing.'

Davies then said that Ninnis had stepped over, 'swiped up' the rock with one hand and hit her on the head with it –

something everyone in court now knew to be impossible. But clearly not for Davies, who said he went on to hit her six or seven times more, now holding the rock in both hands.

'It does not take long to say something,' Mr Taylor said, 'to bring him to his senses. You could see all this happening in front of your eyes, why did you not try?'

'It just happened so quickly,' Davies said.

'Not that quickly,' Mr Taylor answered. 'After the first hit, you say that she was trying to scream but she could not, it was just like a noise. At that point, did you not finally understand what was going on and try to stop him?'

'When you see something like that happen to someone, you do not have an action plan right away,' Davies said. 'If you see someone hit someone with a rock, especially your best friend, you don't act right away.'

'What action plan do you need?' Mr Taylor asked. 'If that had happened, you would have stepped in, wouldn't you? If you are right – if she is not dead because she is trying to scream – do you not say, "Come on, stop it"?'

'I said, "Stop,"' Davies answered. 'I mumbled, "Stop."'

'Was that the best you could do? To just stand there while this attack on someone you supposedly loved took place? Why didn't you say anything else to try and stop him?'

'I was in shock,' Davies replied.

'And why didn't you report it?'

'I didn't think,' he replied.

Such questioning continued, relentlessly. And with each new question that Davies seemed to be struggling to answer, he would get increasingly flustered and agitated. Mr Taylor kept his tone calm, speaking gently and politely but all the while referring to the notes in front of Davies and asking him to go and look at specific pages in order to explain them.

I was beginning to see a side to Davies then that I'd seen countless times but never fully appreciated the implication of: that it felt like the arrogant fury that was typical of psychopaths. In contrast to Mr Taylor's urbane, friendly style, I could see Davies, now he'd been crossed, getting more and more angry, rifling through the sheets with increasing irritation till, at one point, they flew out of his hands altogether and would have fallen to the floor, had he not lunged to grab them. I could all too easily imagine him then, faced with Becca's strength of personality, being enraged in precisely the same way. Except that she had not been a QC in a Crown Court; she'd been a tiny girl, to his 6ft of strapping male muscle. She'd told me, I remembered, how one time she'd seen him beat up a boy and how terrified and disgusted she'd been to witness it. Had she been on the end of such violence, alone with him in the forest? The truth was that he could have swatted her like a fly.

But today it was he who was the victim, which was how it should be. Whatever pleasure I got from seeing him in such a state of discomposure was soon to be replaced by something different, though. Having quizzed him on times and details, Mr Taylor now asked Davies to take him through everything that happened up to the point when Ninnis 'supposedly killed Becca'.

I could see Davies immediately go on the defensive, recognising body language immediately so familiar to me, gripping the inside of his right arm with his left hand in a way I'd seen countless times before. It was as sure a signal to me, as if he'd confessed then and there, and I was only sorry that the jury probably wouldn't recognise its significance. He then did as instructed and re-enacted the whole brutal murder, right down to miming the raising of the rock itself and repeatedly striking Becca. Watching him do that, I broke down – it was all so sickening and shocking. And done with such detachment, even though he was acting it out so enthusiastically, that perhaps even he realised he'd overdone the acting as, when he finished, he actually felt the need to clarify that 'it was Ninnis who did that'.

As I watched Davies give his evidence I remained transfixed by him. Astonished by how well I realised I now knew him. I could see so many little signs, but could the jury? This was not the understandable distress of an innocent, not to mention traumatised teenager, who'd witnessed the brutal murder of a defenceless girl he purported to care about by someone he'd thought was his best friend. No, it was nothing like that. It was the anger of a self-serving, self-absorbed psychopath, one who was furious at having been found out.

At one point I thought he might be broken. He was getting increasingly uncomfortable, flipping angrily though the incriminating list of calls and messages once again, getting more and more flustered because each one was more damning and inexplicable than the last.

Mr Taylor kept the pressure up, politely but relentlessly. He picked up on everything. Asking him about his comment when leaving Ninnis's to meet Becca, he said, 'The time has come. The time has come for *what*?'

Davies failed to provide an answer, so Mr Taylor asked him again. 'Joshua, the time has come for *what*?'

There was another long delay while Davies fidgeted and looked uncomfortable, eventually coming up with, 'They were throwaway comments.'

Mr Taylor ignored this. Instead, he asked again, 'The time has come for *what*?'

The silence stretched and stretched, and we were all on the edge of our seats. Then he finally mumbled, 'To kill her.'

It was the point – the only point so far – when I really thought he might crumble; that Mr Taylor would continue to press him and he'd finally admit what he'd done. But it wasn't destined to happen. It was the end of the day, court was adjourned till the following morning.

I was so upset – I so wanted him to admit to what he'd done. But later, though I didn't realise it at the time, I would be extremely glad that he hadn't that day.

Davies continued to give evidence the following morning and I was pleased to see how attentively the jury seemed to be watching and how several of them were making so many notes. I felt I had come to know them now, even though we had never actually met, and felt this great sense of their commitment to seek out the truth. It must have been the hardest thing imaginable to get papers in the post saying you were going to be doing jury service and then to find out that yours would not be a quick two weeks of minor crimes but a lengthy case that would probably traumatise you greatly. How did it feel on the day when they were told that they'd be responsible for making a decision about such a shocking and barbaric murder? Did it weigh heavily on them? Did they go home to children themselves? Did they lie awake at night, unable to talk to anyone, unable to sleep for thinking about it? Did the images they'd been shown already haunt them and give them nightmares? I didn't know but I hoped – and still hope – that I would one day get the chance to thank them for their incredible dedication.

Mr Taylor was today following a new line of questioning and asked Davies to go to a specific place in his notes, to a text sent that Saturday afternoon.

'Joshua,' he said, 'could you read that for the jurors, please?'

Davies, looking uncomfortable, said, 'M.'

Mr Taylor then explained that Davies had sent that text to the BlackBerry phone (mine) that Becca had on her at around 3pm. 'What does it mean?' he then asked Davies, 'and why did you send it?'

Davies began telling Mr Taylor that he usually kept his phone in his pocket and that it must have been sent by accident because he didn't know he'd sent it and, no, he didn't know what that letter 'M' meant.

I sat and watched him tell this lie incredulously. Davies had an iPhone 4, just as I had, so it was almost inconceivable that he could have sent a text by accident. It was a smartphone with a touch screen and designed so that you couldn't touch it and perform a function without meaning to. To send a text on such a phone, you'd have to press the home key, slide the unlock bar, type your password (Davies had passwords on everything and one of his passwords was 666), touch either 'messages' or 'contacts' and only then, having chosen the recipient and typed the message, would touching 'send' actually transit a message anywhere.

But Mr Taylor didn't press him and though, on one level, it

seemed a missed opportunity – already I'd explained this to the police and it had been noted – on another, his failure to do so was evidence in itself. Mr Taylor was already confident he had enough to convict him.

With the prosecution over, it was time for the defence to make their case, a process that took the rest of that day and went on for the best part of the following week.

Mr Rouch QC tried his very best. He seemed to try everything to help Davies to help himself but it was clear to see that his efforts were largely wasted. There had obviously been discussion about the sort of answers Davies had been coached to give but, time after time – and everyone could see Mr Rouch's frustration – Davies would say something different, answer a question in such a way that only helped to underline his guilt.

It didn't last long, since there was little that could be done in the face of so much overwhelming evidence and much of the defence strategy seemed to take the form of character references, so we sat through countless video-linked testimonies from various friends – most of them girls from other schools in the area, none of whom I recognised or had even known Becca – who seemed to have fallen under Davies's spell. This might not have been the case but, as they recounted tales of drunken parties at his house, it was my overwhelming impression – that and the fact that they had been the lucky ones. With Davies safely in prison, he couldn't murder anyone else.

There were a couple of shocks for me there too, though, as Jess – who'd not been called for the prosecution at all, not even via video evidence – was called as a witness for the defence. I couldn't believe it; how on earth they imagined Jess – Becca's *sister* – could help the defence case was beyond me. I just hoped it was an indication that they were clutching at straws.

Fortunately, it was all over very quickly. They simply played some of the video evidence she'd given down at Coity and, thankfully, didn't call her to be cross-examined on the stand – something I really didn't want her to be put through.

The second shock was that one of the witnesses the defence called in person was Megan James, who'd been one of Becca's best friends in high school and who'd come to our home on so many occasions. I could barely believe, given the weight of the evidence against him, that she had come to support Davies's defence. It felt like a betrayal of Becca and, not for the first time since the trial had begun, I had to leave the court because I was so upset.

On Thursday, 21 July 2011, both the prosecution and defence barristers made their closing speeches to the jury, going over their main arguments and items of evidence and so on. Then, four and a half weeks after the trial had begun, it was time for the judge to sum up the main points and to send the jury out to deliberate. This was it, I realised, as we filed back out of court to return to our waiting room. We could do nothing but sit and wait – well, stand mostly, in my case.

I felt like a caged animal. We couldn't go far from the court and a part of me didn't want to leave the room in any case. Every time any of us did it seemed we were destined to cross the path of one of the Davies family, and whenever it happened to me I'd feel such hate and anger rise inside me; emotions that I found difficult to know how to deal with. I kept thinking of poor Jack, too; how I was having to be away from him so much. I knew he was safe, going to and fro on the school bus, and being looked after so well by my brother Robert, but he needed us home again, for things to return to some kind of normal.

But we were almost there now. We'd known the trial would end today, so we'd all come prepared; we'd brought extra drinks and snacks, as well as reading material, because we had no idea exactly how long we'd have to wait. As with everything else now, it was out of our hands.

In truth, it had *always* been out of our hands. Though we had done all we could to help the police collect evidence, it was the Crown Prosecution Service who had taken Joshua Davies to trial, not our family. So there was never a point when we could influence the course of justice, all we could do was trust that justice would be done.

Davies's fate was now in the hands of those 12 complete strangers who'd sat through almost five weeks of testimony, argument and counter-argument, and had to try and tease the truth about these people they had never met before from the mass of information – and misinformation – they now had.

I had no idea how long that would take them and there was nothing I could do.

Except pray. So I did that, very hard.

CHAPTER TWENTY

THE VERDICT

With murder being such a serious crime, and jury service being such a great responsibility, it would probably have been optimistic to expect the jurors to reach their verdict in the couple of hours left to them when court was adjourned that Friday afternoon. So we weren't surprised when Jill, the usher, came to tell us at around 4pm that day that, as no decision had been reached, court would be adjourned for the weekend and they'd return to deliberate again on the Monday.

So it was that, after a weekend that was drum-tight with tension, we were back in Swansea for 10am on Monday, armed with yet more snacks and things to read, prepared to wait for as long as it took them.

We were there in force – Jess and me, Linda, Roger and his wife, plus several of Becca's closest friends, including Marcus Roberts, who'd come with his mother, Linda, and whose presence there touched me so much. She would have been so proud of him, I knew that; he'd been such a support since day one. One of the first the police had spoken to and, knowing Becca and Davies as well as he had, he knew straight away, without a doubt, who had killed her.

When the jury adjourned for lunch, so did we, going over to the pub restaurant across the road that we'd been in so many times over the past weeks, a place I knew Becca would have approved of as well. It was called The Wig and, as well as having a lovely, welcoming atmosphere, it was full of all things to do with the law – framed wigs and gowns, judges' hammers, briefs and papers and other tools of justice. How much had it seen and heard over the years? I wondered. I imagined it had played host to many other families such as ours, whose lives had been torn apart by violent crimes and were desperately hoping justice *would* be done.

It was here where the usher Jill came over to find us that Monday lunchtime.

'This is it,' I said to Linda, 'they have come to a decision.' I grabbed her hand. 'They're going to call us back into court now, we're going to know.'

But it wasn't: 'I just wanted to let you know what's happening,' Jill told us. 'They're waiting on a question the police need to answer – about that "M" text Davies sent at three in the afternoon to the BlackBerry phone Becca had with her.'

'What do they want to know about it?' I asked her.

'Just whether it had been opened,' she said, 'whether it's been marked as read. Let's hope, whatever the answer, it helps them, eh?'

Though, in fact, once Jill had returned to court, we all discussed it and agreed that we weren't sure in what way it could really help the jury. The facts were clear – it had been sent after Becca was already dead and the phone had been in her bag when they found her the following morning.

So we returned to waiting, sometimes in the pub but mostly sitting in the same waiting room we always had, and, with every coming and going, every barrister that went by, every usher who put his head round the door, we'd think, *This is it, they've reached a verdict.*

And would it be the right one? Everything we'd been told – by the police, by our lawyers, by our legal team – shrieked yes. There was never a point, from the first day, that anyone had doubted it. But would the jury see Davies for what he was, or wouldn't they? Would they be charmed by his innocent-looking 'poor me' expression, or would they have listened carefully to the evidence that incriminated him? I had been sickened throughout, watching how he seemed to smile and joke – how his family seemed to always bring all these children with them, too – and how they sat in court munching on snacks.

I knew he was guilty – had known from the night of Becca's murder, but what if he did walk? What if the lead juror said 'not guilty' and he was free to go – free to trot, grinning that arrogant grin, down the court steps? He wouldn't, that was all – he wouldn't make it to the bottom. Law-abiding, God-fearing person that I was, I knew I would try to tear him limb from limb.

I would be tortured by such thoughts for another two sleepless nights, because it would be Wednesday afternoon before Jill could finally summon us back into court, the jury having reached a majority verdict. And as we filed in, I couldn't stop the thoughts yammering at me. Why had it taken them so long?

My brother Roger kept trying to reassure me. 'It's a good

thing,' he kept saying. 'It means they are going through everything thoroughly, it means the defence will have nothing to complain about.'

Once we were all in court, I could hardly catch my breath. I was so anxious and so was Jess – she was gripping my hand so tightly it hurt. But then the judge entered and asked for the jury to be brought in, then asked if they'd appointed a foreman.

They said they had and when the man stood up, ready to give their verdict, I smiled at Linda – it was the same man we'd agreed at the beginning was the one we hoped they would choose as foreman and it felt like an omen.

Then it was time. And after 19 hours and 55 minutes of deliberation, I heard the words I had only ever expected to hear on a TV show or in a movie.

'Have you reached a verdict?' the court clerk asked the foreman.

'Yes,' replied the foreman, his voice strong, loud and clear.

'And is that verdict guilty or not guilty?' asked the clerk.

Time seemed to stretch then, the silence like a roaring in my ears. My heart was racing so fast, I thought it might burst out of my chest.

The foreman opened his mouth and looked directly at Davies as he spoke. 'Guilty,' he replied.

I heard a cry from beneath us. Davies's mother, I imagined. Davies himself dropped into his seat as if his legs had given way.

I looked across at the jury then, mouthing, *thank you, thank you, thank you.*

Then I clapped until both my hands were burning.

CHAPTER TWENTY ONE

'TOP DOG' NO MORE

Sentencing would take place on 2 September 2011 after the judge had seen various reports, including psychiatric ones, though I was told that the defence weren't going to put up much of a fight now. The judge, who had already told Davies that he would be held at Her Majesty's pleasure and could expect a sentence 'of indefinite duration', now lifted the order that protected him from being identified. Up till now, because of his age, Davies had enjoyed anonymity in the media but the judge lifted the ban because of both the 'strong public interest in open justice' and because he said the community that he had traumatised should know his name. And though the defence had managed to come up with the odd character reference, now that Davies's name was out in the public arena, there were more neighbours venturing forth to give their opinion, all commenting on what a nasty child he'd been and how much trouble he had caused in their street.

In the meantime, I had hoped we'd have a few weeks of peace and quiet – some private time, away from the unending publicity, so we could recover from the ordeal of the trial. How wrong I was. I'd forgotten that I had promised the press that, once the trial was over, I would speak to them.

As we left the court that day, I had wanted to read a statement myself – and had always planned to – but, when the time came, I just couldn't get the words out of my mouth. So, flanked by Jack and Jessica, I stood by while Charmaine read it out to the crowd of journalists and broadcasters who'd been waiting outside the court for me.

In the weeks that followed, I did more interviews – I felt much more comfortable one on one – and I also used the time to prepare a second statement: one that, this time, I was determined I would read out myself.

When the day of the sentencing came, I felt exhausted after yet another sleepless night. I was just so worried that Davies might get a really short sentence; so far away in time from the day he smashed my daughter's skull in, would they take pity and decide to be lenient on him? Would they forget that this was not a one-off, spur-of-the-moment thing he did, but something he had schemed to do for months?

We arrived early because I wanted to be there for every second, my mind racing with conflicting emotions. On the one hand, I wanted him dead – what mother wouldn't? But at the same time, I knew a quick death was too good for him: I wanted him to live and to suffer every day in the same way as we would for the rest of our lives.

There seemed to be police and press everywhere. Uniformed

officers were swarming about all round the court, including those forming a barrier up the steps to the interior. The press, too, were there in force, as we'd expected. This had been a high-profile case and, with such a young defendant found guilty, everyone wanted to know how the courts were going to deal with him. I saw outside broadcast trucks, cameramen and journalists everywhere – BBC, ITV, SKY and several more. It seemed every news network was represented in some way and I knew that, as soon as we emerged after the sentencing, they'd be relaying their stories back to impatient TV and radio channels, and to all the newsrooms for the print media as well.

We, too, were at Swansea Crown Court in great force. All our family, my two Lorraines, Marcus and his mother – still a great support to me – Kayleigh Margetts (Becca's 'Bestest Nerdy Friend', as she would say), Nia Baker, Lauren Richards, Hannah Greenslade and her mum, Jayne, Josh Perkins, Christopher Heath, Helen Stojanovic – so many wonderful friends (and forgive me if I haven't mentioned your name – your support really meant everything). There were also representatives of the police force who'd worked so tirelessly for so many months and to whom we'd grown so close during our time of need – particularly our FLOs, John and Charmaine, who had taken such incredible care of us. I was so glad they were all there with us that day.

Once inside, it was no less frenetic. Security was even tighter than it had been during the trial itself and it took even longer for our bags to be searched. It made me realise that this was, actually, a potentially very dangerous time; that there was always the possibility in a case such as this that someone would try to take the law into their own hands and dispense some rough justice of their own.

I was grateful to be whisked through to our waiting room relatively quickly. And once in there, the police press officer took us through what would happen and I confirmed that I'd prepared a statement to read after sentencing. And then, through the mass of voices, there was a clear one ringing out: they were ready, it was time to go in.

The court, as we'd expected, was packed. There wasn't an empty seat anywhere, as far as I could see, and the public gallery above us was also crammed. So much so that, though legally he was too young to be there, we wanted to take Jack in with us. One of the police officers did try and sneak him in, bless him, but Justice Lloyd Jones saw him and said that, regrettably, he would have to leave. He did ask Jill the usher, however, to see if he could listen to proceedings from the gallery hallway and, once that had been agreed, a uniformed officer took him up there and took care of him for us.

I was also pleased to see the jury in attendance. They felt like friends now and I wished I could personally thank every single one of the jury who had found him guilty. I can only imagine what it must have been like to be them – to have to see and hear, and deliberate on such things. I hoped one day perhaps one or two of them might find me.

The Davies family were ushered in quickly. And within moments, my daughter's killer himself came into court, flanked, as ever, by his guards from Vinney Green. This time he looked different. His hair was darker – no longer worn in his usual blond spikes – but his expression was just as it had ever been. He looked soulless and arrogant, almost completely without emotion, and seemed to be strolling up from the cells almost without a care in the world, as if going to his next class in school.

He thinks he's going to get away with it, I realised with a start, feeling panicky. *Does he know something I don't? Have his defence team reassured him? Is he going be treated leniently because of his age?*

But straight away the judge's demeanour told me otherwise. Even as Davies was being led to his usual seat with his defence team, he ordered that he instead be taken up to the raised dock for sentencing, where everyone in the court could have a clear view of him – and inescapably, he of them. And he would look up to see so many familiar faces; former friends of his, now united in their revulsion for what he'd done, there to see him be told the punishment for his crime.

'I'm so glad he's done that,' Linda whispered beside me. 'He can't hide now. Won't be able to sink in his seat this time either.'

I was glad too because I could see just how difficult he was finding it, having to stand there, looking up into once-friendly eyes that now stared back at him with such loathing and disgust. I could tell because he was now standing in his familiar defensive stance, one arm across his body, clutching the other.

Not so much the self-appointed 'top dog' any more.

And, in the end, justice was done. As my daughter's murderer stood in the dock, growing paler, Justice David Lloyd Jones told him that he was, indeed, to be jailed indefinitely. He added that he would serve at least 14 years before he would be considered for parole and only then when and if he both admitted his crime and showed remorse. And as he passed sentence, he told Davies, 'You have shown yourself to be devious, calculated and controlling. You have shown no remorse. You killed Rebecca in the most brutal way when you struck her repeatedly to the back of her head with a heavy stone, fragmenting her skull. Her death will leave a permanent shadow over the lives of the members of her family, the effect of which has been devastating.'

Once again, Davies began to slump down in the dock, and this time he was crying.

'Get him to stand up,' the judge ordered immediately.

And I was glad. Because everyone in the court knew why he was crying: it wasn't for Becca, it was for himself.

But the most powerful memory of that day – and Linda felt it too – was the sense, the strongest sense, that Becca was standing there beside us, her hands gripping the brass balcony rail, just as ours were, her eyes gazing down on her murderer, just as ours were, and the sense that she knew it – that justice had been done.

EPILOGUE

To lose a loved one is devastating for anyone; to lose your child, the worst nightmare of any parent. To lose your child to a murderer is something so unthinkable that I doubt anyone can bear to contemplate it – I know I never did before we lost Becca.

There is still a great deal we don't know. There are so many unanswered questions, so many items of evidence that I still don't know the significance of, and perhaps I won't, at least for some time to come because the police – unusually, I've been told – are still holding on to everything they collected.

But I am beginning to accept we will probably never know the answers anyway; that only Davies himself holds the key to what made him decide to plan and commit such a barbaric act. I have since spoken to clinicians and the consensus seems to be that he showed strong indications of narcissism and psychopathy, which would mean killing meant little to him emotionally. It would certainly explain his complete lack of emotion when relating his version of events in court.

Why it was Becca who attracted his murderous attentions can only be guessed at. It seems clear, now that I've unearthed so much extra information (in the form of page upon page of MSN conversations between them over many months), that, once he finished dating her, he seemed to have it in for her. The rumours flew – and are still flying – about various unsubstantiated grievances he might have had against her. Not least, the simple fact that, having bragged for so long about getting rid of her, his ego would not allow him to deviate from his path. 'You'll see' – that's what he told Liam Thomas – '*You'll see.*'

But the fact remains that Joshua Davies decided that Becca was some sort of blot on his self-professed 'top dog' copy book; she was doing better than him in school, she was popular and had a boyfriend and perhaps most of all, though she clearly had feelings for him, she was always her own person. Perhaps that annoyed him the most.

But who can say? How do you get inside a mind so obsessed with violence? How do you rationalise human behaviours that are so far from human? Try to understand how a young person – a shockingly young person – could have such determination to end the life of another?

You can't. So there's probably no point in trying. My only hope is that he is never released from prison and put in a position to devise such a plan to kill again.

We would also like to be able to remember our beautiful, gentle Becca, untainted by the stain of her killer's continued existence, as a person to be remembered separately from the evil brutality that brought her life to an end. And as Jack, Jessica and I – not to mention family and friends – try to live our lives without her, it's such a comfort for us to know that she lives on. Some may think I'm mad to believe in an afterlife, but I do – I know she is with me and, most importantly, I know she is safe now: safe in Heaven with my Mam and Dad, where they can look after each other till the time comes when we can all be reunited.

That she can live on through this book is a great comfort too. Hers was a short life, but her time with us was never less than joyful and though she cannot now realise all the hopes and dreams she had, the fact that I have been given an opportunity to share them – and to share what a lovely girl she was – matters greatly to all of us. I am so grateful to have been given the chance to do that.

She will also live on, I hope, through the charity I am setting up in her name, with the intention of helping young driven people, just like Becca, with the costs of things needed for university, to start with, and eventually to help with funding awards for English and English Literature (Becca's favourite subjects) for the best achievers. Her website, https://www.facebook.com/RebeccaOatleyFoundation, is currently under construction. I hope she'll be as proud of it as we are of her.

Bye, Becca. I love you.

VICTIM IMPACT
STATEMENTS

SONIA OATLEY

My name is Sonia Aylward and I'm the mother of Rebecca Sarah Aylward, who was cruelly taken from me on Saturday, 23 October 2010. I would have liked to have read this in court myself so that Joshua Davies could hear directly from me what total devastation he has caused to me and my family, and most importantly, Rebecca. I must start by saying that the pain and horror of losing Rebecca in such a horrendous way is indescribable. I have found it almost impossible to even try to put into words how I feel but I hope that I manage to express at least an idea of what we are going through in this statement.

Life stopped, not just for Rebecca, but for me, Jessica and Jack on that Saturday in October 2010. How do you carry on living after you have lost your fifteen year old child, murdered in such a barbaric, senseless act? Rebecca died, suffering in such a way, at the hands of someone she loved and trusted. I will never forget what he has done to her, or ever forgive him for destroying our family forever.

I was in Pandy park with other family members on the Sunday morning after, having only 45 minutes of sleep the night before as I was up all night phoning Becca. When it kept going to answerphone, each time I got more and more terrified of what might have happened to her. We searched the whole area of where I knew Rebecca had walked while I was speaking to her on the phone. We searched everywhere – including the river – and then the call came from my sister, asking us to go home. There was a police officer waiting to see me. My blood ran cold and I felt sick and numb. I knew my baby was dead. You just know. I was a mother of three beautiful children and now one was gone forever.

I tried to rush back, hoping he was going to say she was injured in hospital but, deep down, you just know. It felt like I was walking through deep mud and I could not go any faster… it felt as though I was being pulled back; the 10 minute journey seemed like an eternity. Everyone was saying that everything would be ok, but I knew: No, it wouldn't, the worst had happened, I knew it had. I sat staring out the window totally numb for the rest of the journey.

When we arrived at my sister's home that morning I ran in and took one look at the officer's face and it said it all. He didn't even have to tell me my child was dead. I felt physically sick and rushed to the bathroom and when I came out I saw Jessica trying to ask the officer things like, 'Are you sure? Can you please try to save her? Have you taken her to hospital?' My thoughts went to my son, who was eight, and how I could tell him. He had been taken to my brother's house, playing with his little cousins, and I needed to tell him before he saw it on TV or someone told him. I was about to shatter his world and tell him Becca was never coming back home. It was the hardest thing I have ever had to do; his little face looking at me in total disbelief as he started shouting at me asking, 'Who did it? Who did it Mam?' I had to tell him, and he said 'No, not Josh, he wouldn't hurt her? You're lying.' And then he broke down sobbing uncontrollably.

There was more to come. I had to go to The Heath in Cardiff to identify my child. They had to cover her head and I stared at her lying there, so small, and her face was so white. They would not let me near her but I wanted to kiss her goodbye and hold her hand so much. Joshua Davies deprived me of that too; I couldn't even have one last kiss or hug because my daughter was a 'crime scene'. Her life brutally cut short at the hands of Joshua Davies – how could he want to do that to her? It was so final.

Rebecca had so much to do. She loved life, her school, her friends and family and she had so much to live for. For most of 2010 she was ill and was hardly ever in school. She was in and out of hospital, having various tests, because she was feeling nauseous and having headaches and was suffering with blackouts for no apparent reason. The doctors at The Princess of Wales Hospital carried out numerous tests on her throughout the months from April to October, including MRI scans, 24 hour heart monitor scans, sleep deprivation tests and numerous blood tests and still they could not get to the bottom of the problem. She was hospitalised in July for observation and more tests and she was too ill to see any of her friends, but some would visit our home to see her.

Rebecca was a sociable girl who had been 'a pleasure to teach' her teachers in both primary and comprehensive schools told me numerous times. It was easy for Rebecca to study because she loved it so much and her teachers loved her for her natural talent and ability in every subject she undertook. She excelled in everything she did and was studying hard to go to University to study Law. From the age of five she wanted to be a solicitor, and then a prosecution barrister, and would say, 'I could never be a defense barrister because I could never defend the guilty'. She would read volumes of law books from a young age, she did work experience in June 2010 in King-Davies & Partners, and worked for Philippa David, a local solicitor. That experience made Rebecca more determined to follow her chosen career, as she thoroughly enjoyed the work there, and King-Davies gave her a very good report for the work that she did for them.

She had her whole life mapped out, even down to the finest details of her wedding; the flowers, the wedding gown and bridesmaid dresses, the designs that she created herself – a day I will never see now. I won't see her walk down the aisle or hug her or her children. I feel as though my heart has been torn out. This has made me so ill and I will never be the same again. I just want to be with my beautiful Becca, but I know I can't. Jessica and Jack need me and I have to stay strong for them. I am afraid to let Jessica and Jack out with their friends, or go to any of their friends' homes. I do not trust anyone anymore, and never will again.

Jessica, too, is extremely nervous and is having great difficulty in sleeping with horrific nightmares about what has happened to her sister. Jessica's education has been severely disrupted because of what has happened, especially with the other boys still at the school and Joshua Davies's brother being in the same year as her. I had to take Jessica out of Archbishop McGrath, as I did not feel it to be safe for her to be there. She went back for a while, but I have decided she will have to leave there permanently now. I am so disappointed with this as she has to leave all the support of her friends and, being a Roman Catholic, I am appalled at the lack of support.

I have had great difficulty sleeping, even though I am physically and mentally exhausted. I take strong medication for a heart condition made worse by what has happened, and all three of us have been diagnosed with PTSD. I have problems concentrating and cannot stay focused. The guilt and torment of not being able to prevent him doing this – I should have been there to stop him doing this to my child – I am overwhelmed with. It just comes over you. Even if you are just out shopping, there is no warning; you just burst into tears with nothing to trigger it. I feel like there is no point to anything anymore. The loss of all your hopes and dreams – everything is so empty. I am still in a state of shock, so traumatised that nothing seems real. It cannot get better. I feel the same now as the day it happened.

Rebecca was intelligent, kind and sensitive, always ready to help others. She worshipped her younger brother Jack and sister Jessica and she was always there for them to play and help to look after them. They looked up to their 'big sis', as they would call her. Now they have been left traumatised by what has happened and have to see psychiatrists, probably for many years to come, as they have shut themselves away from their friends. There is no trust anymore for anyone.

Joshua Davies betrayed not only Rebecca but me, Jessica and Jack. He promised Becca he would never let anyone harm her. He told me he would take care of her. Joshua Davies let us all down. Jack is so devastated that Josh did this; he goes into Rebecca's bedroom every single night before bed to say goodnight to her and kisses her photo and sobs uncontrollably and asks me, 'why, Mam?' What do I say to him? Not only has he taken Rebecca from me, but I have the agony of seeing my two other children suffer with the loss of their sister that they love and miss so much. He has destroyed my entire family and turned our lives upside down, and I will never forgive him for that. If he has a shred of humanity left he should at least admit what he has done and why. I still wonder, if Jack had gone with Rebecca that day as planned would he have done the same to him?

Rebecca was so small, dainty and gentle. She cared for the whole family, especially all her little cousins, as she was the oldest and they all looked up to her. But now they keep asking, 'Where is she?' How do you explain this to them: they are only three, four and six years old. Now they see her photos in newspapers and point out and say 'Becca'.

She always had time for everyone, especially her friends, always supporting them and giving them practical help in solving their problems, very often on the phone or laptop until the early hours if need be. One of her favourite sayings was 'Never go to bed on a bad note', and she would ensure that would never happen. Rebecca loved to shop, especially for clothes and shoes, and wanted shops to stay open 24/7. She loved going to restaurants with family or friends, liked long walks on the beach and we would just walk and talk for hours. Life is so empty now, without her at home. There are hours of silence, where it used to be filled with the sound of my three children laughing, singing and dancing together. Now we have tears and sadness – and no Rebecca to help us through it. Life will never be the same again. It is forever night, always dark, our light has gone out forever.

We welcomed you, Josh, as part of our family, and you repay us with this evil, despicable, horrific act that is totally inexcusable. And you will have to answer to it one day. Your contempt for a human life is just beyond comprehension. Being a 'Roman Catholic' obviously means nothing to you especially as you didn't take your oath on the Bible, which I did, because I told the truth with God as my witness.

I have sat in court for the last five harrowing weeks, hoping you would give me an answer to why you did this to my child, trying to find out what happened, but you have lied in court and have refused to tell the truth. Why could you not tell me? I still want to know. Why did you violate, terrorise and murder *my* defenceless child?

You know the atrocities that you have committed. Your attitude and apparent lack of remorse shows us that you have no conscience at all. You even spent most of your time laughing during proceedings. You are a danger to my family, after your threat to Jessica at her birthday party. She will be living the rest of her life in fear of you if you ever get released.

The amount of planning you put into murdering my child proves what an evil, callous person you are and you should never be given the opportunity to do it again. Because you would do it again, to another innocent child, you are very capable of re-offending and putting members of the public in grave danger. Therefore I hope that you will be refused parole in the future, for the safety of my younger daughter, and the public in general. I would hate for another family to go through the torment I have had to endure and for those reasons I would like my comments recorded for future reference.

Many of Rebecca's friends have taken the time to tell us how much Becca had touched their lives and have created memorials for her. I would like to thank all of you who have sent hundreds of cards and letters and for your constant support and prayers throughout these past dreadful months.

I especially wish to thank South Wales Police, in particular Charmaine Kinson, John Doherty, Carol Saunders, John Penhale, and the rest of the Major Crime Unit. Also thanks to Ross Mather.

I am also extremely grateful for the meticulous presentation of the prosecution case by Mr Gregg Taylor QC, & Mr Thomas Crowther.

JESSICA OATLEY

It feels like every day is a struggle to keep going on. Life without Bec is unbearable; I have seen how much it has affected me and my family. There's always these awkward moments which, when Bec was here, she would be able to fill. It feels as if my whole life has been ruined, turned upside down, and will never be the same again. The day the police came to tell us, my world was shattered. I kept asking the police officer, 'Are you sure it's Becca? Can you try to save her? Is she in hospital?' I could not stop crying and, when I went home, seeing my Mam and Jack that upset made it even worse. We cried all night until we all fell asleep, hugging each other.

There's still this sense of fear that I have, that Liam Thomas and Daniel Ninnis have something against me and my family. I walk past them in school and put my head down and pretend I haven't seen them. I actually try not to make eye contact, just in case they come up to me or do something irrational. I hate the fact that I walk around looking over my shoulder, wondering if they want to kill me too! I'm sick of being treated as if I have done something wrong, and what I mean is, instead of Jordan Davies, Liam Thomas, Tyler Harry and Daniel Ninnis moving schools, I have to: it's not fair. I have moved twice now in the space of about six months. I have moved twice because I feel intimidated and scared of each and every one of those boys. It seems like, wherever I go, they are there too. I can walk up to the venders in school for a drink or something to eat, and there they are laughing with one another and all their friends. It seems to me as if all that has happened is just one big joke to them all.

This has affected me in so many ways. I actually dread going to sleep, because I keep having nightmares about everything that has happened. I have even had dreams about how I was Becca that day. I wake up in a sweat, crying and feeling like I'm about to be sick.

Every morning I wake up and go straight into Bec's room, just checking if all of this is one big, horrible dream. Then, every night, I go into her room to say goodnight and tell her how much I love her and how much I miss her.

I think about what has happened every day and cannot get those thoughts out of my head. I just can't see me ever being happy or actually living normally after this. There's no way I can get over all this and carry on. How am I supposed to move on with my life knowing that my sister isn't even here? I don't have my big sister to go to for advice or with questions or help me with anything. So how can I carry on living normally without my sister guiding me through everything?

I can never do anything or say anything without being reminded by something of Bec. She was always there for me when I needed her, and we would tell each other everything. No matter what happens now, I'm still not going to get my sister back. Sometimes I do think to myself, after all the trial is finished and everything is done with, how is it going to make that much of a difference, because Bec still isn't here? And what happens if Joshua Davies is ever released? After the threats he made to me and the time he pulled that knife on me and Becca stopped him… I can't see anything stopping him from doing it again now and what if he actually use it on me this time? I will be looking over my shoulder for the rest of my life, wondering if he is out there. Whoever reads my statement in the future, please don't let him out, because he will do it again.

This has also affected my social life, too. I'm not allowed out to my friend's houses anymore, they have to come to my house. I'm missing out on school trips because of the trial and the fact that Jordan Davies might be there. I don't see my friends as often as I used to and I don't see how that is fair on me at all.

I can't face going back to Archbishop knowing that all those boys are still there. I find it a bit strange that the head teacher won't get them out of the school. That's why I have had to move twice in one year. I feel like I'm in the wrong.

After everything that has happened, I feel as if I can *never* trust anyone in my life again. Well at the end of the day, I trusted Joshua Davies, and look what happened there? I don't see how I'm ever going to let my guard down to anyone but my Mam and little brother Jack. Even some of my best friends I'm still wary of. I can't trust *anyone* but my mother and brother now!

I'm terrified of Joshua being let off on parole or being released, because I know he will come for me. He must have something against me and my family, but I know that I'm next. If he ever comes out on parole it looks like I will have to move or something because I'm that scared of him. I have nightmares about him coming out of prison, and the first thing he does is comes for me. I am so scared of him coming out.

I don't think about one minute goes past when I don't think about my sister. Then, as I get upset, I have this enormous amount of guilt come over me, thinking that maybe if I had gone with her that day, I might have been able to stop it. But then again, would he have done it to me too? I guess we will never know now. Only two people know exactly what happened that day, and that's him and Bec. It doesn't seem as if he is going to tell anyone what happened that day.

I still talk about Bec as if she's still here, like my mother will say something and I will say something like, 'I'll have to tell Bec that later!' Then there's this silence that goes on for ages, and I hang my head, fighting to keep the tears back, knowing my mother is over the other side of the room doing the same.

I get frustrated every time I think of Joshua. Knowing that he's just sitting there, with no sorrow at all. While my sister could be here right now, studying for her exams. She had such high potential in life, and every single teacher always said 'she could have easily made it to whatever she wanted to achieve'. It's just such a waste of such amazing talent.

Most mornings I just don't want to get up from bed, knowing that I have another day of pain and misery. I don't want to speak to anyone some days. I just want to sit down and shut the whole world off. But I know that's not what Bec would want me to do. She would always tell me to never give up, to carry on fighting until the very end. And that's exactly what I'm going to do; I'm going to keep fighting every distressing, stubborn day. And I'm going to do it for Bec.

We haven't even been given time to grieve properly, because, as soon as it happened, we had to worry about the funeral and had to plan all of that, and then after the funeral we had to start thinking about the trial and everything! It's unbelievably stressful all the time with everything.

It's actually coming up to a year in a couple of months. But I can still remember it like it was yesterday. I remember the feeling in my stomach as we went to look for her. The feeling of panic and terror and dread all in one, but still even then I tried my best to think that she was going to turn up. As we walked through Aberkenfig that morning, it was almost like I knew what was going to happen. I almost knew that, because she hadn't answered her phone or anything, something truly bad had happened. I was definitely right.

We all knew something was wrong when Bec hadn't answered her phone. Because no matter where she was or who she was with she would *always* answer her phone. And if she didn't she would have a good reason like it ran out of battery or something like that. I always believed Bec, because I don't think she ever lied to me.

I know that it must be hard for whoever is reading this to actually understand how much people loved Bec, because all you know about Becca is what people say and what you read really. But I can't really describe her in words. She is such a kind, loving, cheerful, beautiful girl! And I will miss her forever and love her forever!

LORRAINE SURRINGER, ENGLISH TEACHER, ARCHBISHOP MCGRATH

I first met Rebecca Oatley (Aylward) when she was a Year 7 pupil in Archbishop McGrath School. I am a supply teacher and Archbishop is one of the schools I teach in most frequently. At the time I was covering her English class for a number of weeks. I introduced myself and at some point in the lesson I noticed this shy, pretty girl raise her hand to speak to me. She told me her grandmother's name was Surringer, the same as my own, and we subsequently discovered that we were, in fact, distantly related.

Over the following five years I got to know Rebecca (Becca) well because she stood out as a gifted young student. Her standard in English was excellent, but she was also a joy to teach due to her quiet yet enthusiastic approach to her work. She rarely needed any individual help and I never had to speak to her concerning problems with her work or attitude. She was diligent and very quiet in class – she just got on with it and her work was always of a high standard. I was confident that she would excel in whatever career path she chose in the future. I believe that she wanted to follow a career in law – and I am certain she would have been an asset in this field.

The last time I conversed with Becca in the weeks prior to her tragic loss, she had been a victim of ill health and had missed some school and her main concern was the effect it might be having on her education. I tried to reassure her that she would have no worries as far as her English was concerned.

This young lady was an absolute joy to teach and know. She was quiet and studious but I could see that she was very popular with her friends. She had all those qualities that make a good friend. I have seen for myself the grievous effect her loss has had on her family, friends and those around her. I have experienced for myself the same effect. I have never been so traumatised by a loss and never a day goes by when I don't think about Becca and the injustice of it all. This girl would have contributed so much to society and helped to make the world a better place. I just can't believe that anyone could have wanted to harm her as she was so gentle and kind herself. It makes no sense.

GOODBYE

Dear Becca,

We all miss you so much, big sis, it just gets harder each day that goes by. We would do anything to change that day, for sure. I wish I was there to try to protect you. I would have tried my best to stop it happening.

I always think about how I wished I stopped you going that day, but it's all too late.

I wish I could see you for a few moments at least, I would do anything for that. We always used to have so much fun and play about and laugh a lot, but it is so different now. It's not the same anymore, and that is so unfair.

I still go in your room. Everything is still there, all your favourite teddies and jewellery. I can still smell your perfume, so I know you are still looking after me. We always talk about you every day and there is never a day that goes by without me thinking about you, and it's the same for everyone else too.

I remember how happy you were that Saturday, you were singing and dancing with me in the lounge and you were happier than ever. I loved that, it made me smile to see you like that, especially after being that ill for all those months and in hospital.

You were like a second Mother to me, always there for me, looking after me. We have so many photos of me and you and you always had your arm around me or holding my hand. I remember you reading me stories and singing me to sleep when I was a baby. I watched the videos the other day. There are so many things we did together and I will never forget those days

You are always remembered I will always miss you

Rest in peace Angel

Love you xx

Jack xxxxxxx

When I started writing this book, I didn't realise it would be one of the hardest things I have ever had to do. Reliving losing Becca over and over again in the words that I was writing, stopping many times because I could not see through the tears streaming down my face, going to and fro among chapters because I could not deal with writing certain chapters at that time, the many nights when I could not sleep due to the thoughts running through my mind or fear of having 'that nightmare' again so that I would have to get up and write – I needed to put all the wrongs and lies Joshua Davies told in court right. I had to tell *you* the readers the truth.

How cold, callous and cruel Davies was. He spent so much time with us and he was part of our family. We welcomed him like one of our own. Little did we know we had a murderer living under our roof who would betray us in the most brutal of ways. On numerous occasions he stayed over for many days at a time... was he planning his vicious attack while I cooked his food? What evil thoughts were going through his mind while he was sitting there watching a movie? It chills me to the bone to think back to those times and how he could have wiped my whole family out in one of the many nights he stayed over, and I with no idea of what that monster was planning.

It was difficult for me afterwards because I had to throw away so many things; his favourite pint glass, the sofa and chairs he sat on, almost anything he had contact with. He had left his pink gloves and other things like headphones and a toy dinosaur at our home. I gave them to the police. I wanted no trace of his evil in my home.

After murdering my daughter, he put us through even more torment with the trial. It felt like he wanted to see us all suffer more and, when that was over, I was relieved that he was behind bars. But only for fourteen years! Less than a year for each year my child had lived; Becca was only fifteen and her life was just beginning.

His sentence felt like an insult, as life should mean life: he forfeited his own life when he chose to take my daughter's. No other family should go through the pain and torment that we are still suffering and I worry that he will do it again. He threatened Jessica and in my opinion he is a danger to the public and should never be released I have told my concerns to the police and the media and I hope they take my words seriously.

On the subject of the press, I know so many people complain about them, but I have to say they have given us privacy when we needed it most and respected our wishes throughout, and I thank them all for that. I would particularly like to thank Helen Callaghan, who was brave enough to ask the judge to release Joshua Thomas Davies's name in the interest of the general public, to which he agreed. Davies is cruel and evil and I will never be able to forgive him.

They say 'time is a great healer'. It is not true. Whoever said that has never lost a child. Perhaps in the process of losing parents or grandparents things will get better over time, as that is expected, but to suffer the pain of losing your child… nothing compares to it and there's no way you could prepare for it. You feel the physical pain of having your heart ripped out, a huge part of what you are is not there anymore, and it never leaves you. It's constantly there, taking a little bit more each day, prolonging the agony and adding to the physical pain you feel. You face a daily battle with the mental torture of what happened, reliving in vivid detail and images every minute of that day. With sleep (if you are able) comes the horrendous nightmares: I still have them, they will never go away… My children have them still, too, and I feel powerless to help them. I wish I could take their pain away but I can't; they have to live the rest of their lives trying to cope with the devastating loss of their beautiful big sister, who they idolised, who they were so close to. The hurt is especially there on remembering family days when they were inseparable: their excited little faces as they loaded their backpacks with snacks, drinks, books and toys ready to take with them. Thankfully, I have thousands of photos and many videos of our days out that we can look back on, so that they will never forget the great times they had.

Rebecca being the first child, from the moment she started talking she was her own person. She didn't have a brother or sister to look up to or imitate and she created her own individual style, quite old-fashioned but yet grown up and oh-so-clever. Even a bit bossy, in a comical way, with her mass of curls and rosy cheeks (she wouldn't like me saying that she didn't like the rosy cheeks), she loved dressing up in pretty dresses with co-ordinating hat, bag and shoes and would always keep them like new. I could dress her in anything as a small child and often, in the summer, beautiful white summer dresses and white sandals – we could be out all day, down at the beach, shopping, in restaurants and, even after eating lunch with chocolate ice cream or fudge cake, her dress would look the same as when she put it on. She loved her clothes, a real shopaholic. I still have all her clothes (some with the tags still on that she didn't get chance to wear) in her white wardrobe that she insisted on building herself.

And boy could she talk! Once she started she never stopped. Her primary school rang me one day and said they were concerned that she wasn't finishing her lunch in time because she wouldn't stop talking! She had a unique and distinct voice, and always spoke with conviction. When she was in high school she took to other languages like a duck to water. When she went to France on a school trip she went to a shop to buy pastries and Becca had no problem talking with him, even translating for everyone else in the shop as well.

Her thirst for knowledge and the endless amount of books she read, usually two books at a time, meant she always strived to be the best, and her school reports stated that she excelled in all her subjects. She had her life meticulously mapped out, down to the colour and design of bridesmaid's dresses and her bouquet, but now we have been deprived of all of those special days. I will never be a grandmother to Rebecca's children (she had even chosen their names!).

When Becca was at home there was never a quiet or dull moment. She filled our home with happiness and her constant chatter – even in her sleep I could have a conversation with her! I would always check in on the children at night, and she would sit up in bed, rattling away. I would always put my hand under her head and lay her back down saying 'Go back to sleep now, Angel' and she would go back to dreaming, probably about shopping.

Now our light has gone out and our home has fallen silent.

Our lives will never be the same again. Becca is so dearly loved and missed by us all, and not just the family. Her friends have been left devastated by losing her, and have made paintings and sketches of her and sent them to me. I am currently setting up The Rebecca Oatley foundation in her name and will also be fundraising to help other children and young adults to achieve all of the things Becca wanted to do in her life. I think she would approve. I also want to work with victims who are going through the same trauma as we are, ideally work alongside family liaison officers who cannot always answer the questions that victim's families need to know the answers to.

If I can achieve these things to help Rebecca's name live on, and keep her memory alive, and if we can help anyone through our work at the Foundation, I know it would make Becca proud.

I miss you, and love you so much Rebecca xxx

Until we meet again.

Forever in our Hearts.

Mam xxx

Let it Never be Forgot

Links to my pages and other organisations who have helped me and other victims of homicide:

Becca's foundation page:
https://www.facebook.com/RebeccaOatleyFoundation
Dedicated to this book:
https://www.facebook.com/sonia.oatley.byemamiloveyou
My contact page: https://www.facebook.com/sonia.aylward
A page about Joshua Davies:
https://www.facebook.com/pages/Joshua-Davies-Must-never-be-released-from-prison/283858038314265
My petition to get justice for Becca:
https://you.38degrees.org.uk/p/Justice-for-Rebecca
My petition to get life sentences to mean life in prison for murder: http://www.petitionbuzz.com/petitions/alife4alife
http://www.childbereavement.org.uk/
http://www.victimsfirst.org.uk/
http://www.aafda.org.uk/
Families fighting for justice:
https://www.facebook.com/groups/125298696921/
Mothers Against Murder And Aggression (MAMAA):
http://www.mamaa.org/
The Aim Of MAMAA:
'To Provide An All Inclusive Practical/Emotional Support & Advocacy Service to Those Affected by Serious Violent Crime & Homicide'. They are a truly excellent organisation who have helped me with so many issues.